More about *Covered Calls and Naked Puts* and *The Money Tree*

I highly recommend *Covered Calls and Naked Puts* by Ronald Groenke. It is an excellent supplemental text for finance courses. The book does a fine job of illustrating how writing options can be used to enhance the returns on a common stock portfolio. The real world context in which the story unfolds is a critical advantage, allowing students to observe a derivatives strategy in a practical application. **Professor J. Howard Finch,**
Ph.D. Eminent Scholar in Finance, Florida Gulf Coast University.

I read *Covered Calls and Naked Puts* last night. Congratulations! Have not enjoyed an academic book this much since reading *The Goal* by Goldratt, 15 years ago. I found myself into the story, wanting to get a pencil and paper, find a calculator, grab a *Wall St Journal*, and get to work making money. The story line is subtle and believable. The covered call explanation is clear and a logical development of the formulas. The examples blend into the construction of the total theory of making money via covered call technique. This could be a "How to . . ." book or an academic supplement to a hedging/financial instruments course. **Dr. Bob Cluskey**
CPA, Professor of Accounting, State University of West Georgia

What a great read. Explains in simple-to-understand language that leads you step by step to easily pick profits off of "The Money Tree." Don't know what to call the book. Practical. Ingenious. Magical. Actually, all of these—and many more like them—are perfect fits. If you are looking for a sure-fire way to substantially improve your investment return (almost without risk), *Covered Calls and Naked Puts* is like finding the Holy Grail. **Irving L. Blackman**
CPA Lawyer, Bank Board Chairman, Author.

I have enjoyed gratifying returns in my covered call writing since reading your book, *The Money Tree: Risk Free Options Trading*, and modifying my trading rules to reflect the principles adduced in the book. The software I purchased from you was helpful in winnowing out the overwhelming number of possibilities for trades and in illustrating the real-world relationship among stock price, options premium, and time to expiration. Good luck with your new book! **Al Hackney, II**
CPA, Naples, Florida

I was a real novice at options trading. The basic approach outlined in the book was easy to understand and a great introduction. I use the software for the simulation to deepen my understanding and the Magic Chart has become an indispensable guide. **Narin Anderson**
Eden Prairie, Minnesota

My brother and I started using Ronald Groenke's strategies and softw~~~ February of 2003. Both my brother and I have ma~~~ first year. We are still refining our methods ~~~

buy, but feel we have a good start with this strategy. We finally don't have to rely on the latest hot tip from a broker or financial news letter. We find the stocks, we find the options, we succeed or fail on our own. The best part of the strategy is I don't have to pay any employees, (We are business owners with over 100 employees) or any employee benefits and still make over 40% return on my investment. Thanks for the easy to understand strategy. We spend five to ten hours per week on research but it is well worth the effort!

Ralph and Rob Zimmerman
Ames, Iowa

The Money Tree software package is an indispensable tool to aid in understanding and trading options. It is very user-friendly and easy to learn the program. It has the capability to help identify prospects, manage a list of prospects, and help to determine the risk vs. reward of any potential trade. As a user of the Money Tree software package for over a year, I would highly recommend it to you.

Dr. Ed Rumberger
Naples, Florida

I not only use the Money Tree software on a regular basis but I have recommended it to several of my friends interested in beginning with options. They report it is easy to use, identifies good prospects, and provides them with confidence that they can use options wisely. I feel like a hero, thanks to Ron Groenke.

Gary Sigler
Spokane, Washington

The Money Tree is a fabulous easy to read explanation of the covered call process. Adding naked puts is a very logical extension and a most interesting strategy. The software program is easy to navigate and a definite aid to the process of writing covered calls efficiently and effectively . . . I highly recommend it.

Stephen M. Bean
Host Entrepreneurial Focus Radio Show, Detroit, Michigan

The Money Tree Software Toolset is a NO-BRAINER if you are serious about using the valuable information found in The Money Tree text. For the value you get out of the software, Wade and Ronald are practically giving it away. Do yourself a favor and get the software now . . . you'll be glad you did!"

Dr. Trevor Van Wyk
Littleton, Colorado

I found The Money Tree great reading with a very interesting style that is so very different from other investment books. In the end I did write some covered calls following the software you provided and was very successful. I have been investing for over 30 years and the Money Tree prompted me to finally write a covered call. Why did I wait so long? I look forward to your new book Covered Calls and Naked Puts: Create Your Own Stock Options Money Tree. Thanks for prompting me to move ahead with writing covered calls and making more money.

Dick Stroble
Safety Harbor, Florida

COVERED CALLS
AND **NAKED PUTS**

*Create Your Own Stock
Options Money Tree*

Ronald Groenke

KELLER PUBLISHING
Marco Island, Florida

ISBN 0-9674128-9-7

Printed in the United States of America

Published by

KELLER PUBLISHING

590 Fieldstone Dr.

Marco Island, FL 34145

KellerPublishing.com

To my lovely wife Vergeane (Jean)
who has been a great inspiration in all of my
projects and has brought me happiness.

Acknowledgment

Thanks to my friend, Wade Keller, who has also been my editor and publisher. It was at a Rotary Club meeting several years ago that I gave a presentation on my stock options strategy. After the meeting Wade said, "Ron, you've got a book there." That was the beginning of the process that led to this book.

I would also like to acknowledge and give a heartfelt thanks to Wade's wife, Sue, for her interest and friendship.

Disclaimer

There is a high degree of financial risk when trading in the stock and options market. The author and publisher stress that it is possible to lose money that is invested in these markets. The methods and techniques presented in this book may be profitable or they may result in a loss. Past results are not necessarily indicative of future results. The examples of specific companies that are used in this book are only for informational purposes and are not recommendations.

This publication is sold with the understanding that the author and publisher are not engaged in providing legal, accounting, or other professional services. If legal advice or other expert assistance is required, the services of a competent professional should be sought. Although every precaution has been taken in the preparation of this book, the publisher and author assume no liability for errors and omissions. This book is published without warranty of any kind, either expressed or implied. Furthermore, neither the author nor the publisher shall be liable for any damages, either directly or indirectly arising from the use or misuse of the book.

Before investing, learn as much as you can about the investments that you plan to make. Do extensive research. Knowledge will put the odds in your favor.

Contents

Preface

Let's say you own some blue chip stock. Do you realize that you could sell a call option at a stock price higher than the current price and earn five to six percent on your holdings in three months or even ten percent in six months? There is no additional risk. You have already assumed the risk of stock ownership. After selling CALL options, if the stock goes up enough your stock gets called (you sell it) at a price you specified. If the stock stays about the same or goes down, the CALL option expires. In either case you pocket the money (premium) generated by selling the option.

Company/ Stock	Stock Price 3/17/04	Call Option Strike Month	Call Option Strike Price	Call Option Symbol	Call Option Premium	% Gain if Sold	% Gain if Expired
Intel	27.52	Apr	27.50	INQDY	1.20	4.29	4.36
(INTC)		Jul	27.50	INQGY	2.25	8.10	8.18
Siebel Sys	11.15	May	12.50	SGQEV	0.45	16.14	4.04
(SEBL)		Aug	12.50	SGQHV	0.90	20.18	8.07
Gen Elec	30.53	Jun	30.00	GEFF	1.85	4.32	6.06
(GE)		Sep	30.00	GEIF	2.35	5.96	7.70
RF Micro	8.88	May	10.00	RFZEB	0.40	17.12	4.50
(RFMD		Aug	10.00	RFZHB	0.75	21.06	8.45
Walmart	58.74	Jun	60.00	WMTFL	1.90	5.38	3.23
(WMT)		Sep	60.00	WMTIL	3.00	7.25	5.11

In the chart above, first example, you could receive $1.20 per share on your Intel stock for an option lasting one month, expiring in April. That's a return of 4.3% for one month. If you are willing to let the option expire in July you receive, immediately, $2.25 per share. The premium is yours regardless of whether the option expires or is exercised.

Maybe you would like to buy a blue chip stock but not at the current price. Did you know someone would pay you while you wait for the price to go down? By selling a PUT option you pick the price and time frame for your willingness to invest. If the price of the stock goes down to your desired price you buy the stock. If the price stays about the same or goes up the PUT option expires. Again in either case you pocket the money (premium) generated by selling the option. A put option that is three months out could return four to five percent of the stock purchase price, or even eight percent for waiting six months.

Company/ Stock	Stock Price 3/17/04	Put Option Strike Month	Put Option Strike Price	Put Option Symbol	Put Option Premium	% Dis-count	New Stock Price if Assigned
Intel	27.52	Apr	25.00	INQPE	0.30	1.20	24.70
(INTC)		Jul	25.00	INQSE	1.00	4.00	24.00
Siebel Sys	11.15	May	10.00	SGQQB	0.40	4.00	9.60
(SEBL)		Aug	10.00	SGQTB	0.80	8.00	9.20
Gen Elec	30.53	Jun	27.50	GERY	0.45	1.64	27.05
(GE)		Sep	27.50	GEUY	0.90	3.27	26.60
RF Micro	8.88	May	7.50	RFZQU	0.25	3.33	7.25
(RFMD		Aug	7.50	RFZTU	0.55	7.33	6.95
Walmart	58.74	Jun	55.00	WMTRK	1.20	2.18	53.80
(WMT)		Sep	55.00	WMTUK	2.20	4.00	52.80

Again for example, considering Intel in the chart above you would receive $1.00 for each share you agree to buy for $25.00 per share through expiration date in July. Of course you would only be "put" the stock if it is below $25.00 at the end of that period. In either case, as with calls, you receive and keep the premium. For WalMart you would receive $2.20 per share if you agree to be put the stock at a price of $55 per share through September expiration.

The concepts and techniques in this book have been proven in actual practice. The author has executed these types of transactions over the past eighteen years and has the account history to back up the principles in this publication. Actual account trading results can be reviewed that will demonstrate that you can more than double your money in three years with covered calls and naked puts.

These concepts are available for anyone to use. The problem is that most investors, even most financial advisors, do not understand the advantage of using options to enhance portfolio performance. If the additional returns on your investment seem unreal after you have implemented some of the strategies in this book, great for you. You keep the rewards of your new investment skills and I have the satisfaction knowing that I was able to advance your financial well being.

Introduction

by Jerome Tuccille

Ronald Groenke has written a gem of a book that is ideal for conservative investors looking for low-risk opportunities in the options market. For most investors, the options market is an arcane universe populated by puts and calls, spreads and straddles, and other unfathomable concepts. The author has done an admirable job of de-coding the mysteries surrounding these investment products and rendering them comprehensible to average investors. Most people who are unfamiliar with options regard them as highly speculative and specialized tools for sophisticated investors. What is largely overlooked is that, for every free-wheeling investor who speculates on puts and calls, there is a conservative investor on the other side of the trade who uses options to generate extra income for his or her portfolio. *Covered Calls and Naked Puts* addresses the conservative side of the options market.

This book offers one of the *best* expositions of low-risk options trading I've ever read. I was particularly impressed by the stock-picking advice and discourse on how to find value in puts and calls.

Also valuable is the so-called "Cedric Chart" on historical stock market highs and lows, which at first glance appears deterministic, but is primarily reflective of boom and bust cycles in the past and serves as a suggested roadmap for the future.

The author leads the reader by the hand through the basics of the most conservative options strategies, such as selling covered calls and selling puts on stocks one would like to own. By the time investors are finished absorbing the information contained in *Covered Calls and Naked Puts*, they will feel comfortable embarking on the strategies discussed, with the goal of generating extra income in their accounts on a regular basis. As an investment professional with 30 years experience in the financial services industry, I wholeheartedly recommend this book.

Jerome Tuccille is the author of 21 books, including *How to Profit From the Wall Street Mergers, Rupert Murdoch,* and *Alan Shrugged.*

1

The Money Tree

"Why not go out on a limb. That's where the fruit is."
Will Rodgers

"Jake!" Katie Kimball finally got her husband's attention. Before selling Kimball CPA Firm and retiring to south Florida, Jake could be counted on to be out of the house and at the office at least 10 hours a day.

Looking up from the early edition of the New York Times Book Review Jake quietly replied, "Yes, dear?"

"I said, 'Are you going to Rotary today?' And now that I've got your attention would you mind not scattering your newspapers all over the floor. And by the way the Petersons are just back from the Alaska cruise. I saw Lori at Walgreens and she was driving a new BMW convertible. So cute. Their son has graduated from Bowdoin and is accepted at Harvard Law School. Now if you are going to Rotary I will press that new shirt I got for you at Goodwill. But if you are not going we should go walk on the beach because it's low tide now and you know. . ."

The phone rang and Jake quickly retreated again to the safe environment of the book reviews. Before he could find where he had left off the worrisome thoughts came again. He laid the paper down and looked out the window at the areca palms they had planted as a border across the back of their modest home only three blocks from the beach. He had sold the CPA firm too soon and for too little. In their mid fifties they had moved to the pleasant community of Marco Island with plans to write the *Great American Novel* and get it published before their savings ran out. A recent statement from their investment advisor had shown that funds in the retirement account were getting dangerously low. And unless he finished the novel, that was all they had to live on.

These thoughts were never far from his mind. His wife's comments about his new shirt from the Goodwill store and the conspicuous consumption by their friends, Lori and Steve Peterson, had caused his financial concerns to come roaring back to the surface. He needed to do something. Take action. He glanced quickly at his watch and his coffee cup. A command decision was required. Yes! Plenty of time for another cup of coffee before going to Rotary.

***

Jake stood in awe. Like an appreciative artist admiring a Rodin sculpture, he stood looking at the most beautiful Mercedes Benz he had ever seen. Long and powerful, it made a statement of elegant practicality. It had caught his attention as he was about to enter the Olde Marco Inn for the Rotary luncheon. He enjoyed the Marco Island Rotary Club. It was a close-knit, fun group and he knew all the members. Several owned expensive cars. Scott's Rolls Royce came to mind. He was curious wondering which of his friends had acquired the new Mercedes.

The invocation and pledge of allegiance to the flag were followed by introduction of guests. Looking across the room Jake saw his friend Steve Peterson stand up to introduce a guest who looked vaguely familiar. The visitor reminded him of a college professor from years ago. What was the name? Graham? Yes that was it. Professor Robert Graham. But that's not likely he thought. After all he hadn't seen the professor in over 30 years.

His mind easily slipped back to a particular scene from his college days. He had pulled frantically into the parking lot, already five minutes late for his first class of the semester. It was a hot fall day at the University of Minnesota. As he grabbed his books from the back seat he noticed another car jerk to a stop in the vacant slot next to him. Steam was billowing from under the hood and the car was generally banged up. Jake noticed the windshield had a long crack. Apparently the driver's side door wouldn't open because the young man slid across the front seat and quickly out the passenger side with brief case in hand.

"Can I help you?" Jake had asked, concerned that the car might catch on fire.

Noticing Jake for the first time, the man quickly said, "Hi. Sorry, don't have time to chat. I'm running late for class. Old Betsy will be OK once she cools off. Powerful thirst." With that the man raced into the building.

As Jake made his way to the classroom he was surprised to see the owner of the old clunker standing at the lectern. Finding a seat Jake noticed the professor had a pleasant smile and twinkle in his eyes as he said to the class, "Welcome to Finance 101. My name is Robert Graham. Don't call me doctor yet as I still have a little work to do on my Ph.D. dissertation. Just call me professor."

"We have a former Rotarian. A Paul Harris Fellow." The sound of Steve Peterson's commanding baritone voice brought Jake back to the present. "My special guest today has a suite on the same floor at my condominium. We met on the elevator this morning and, spur of the moment, I invited him to join us for lunch. Please give a warm Rotary welcome to a new resident of Marco Island, Dr. Robert Graham."

After the meeting Jake wasted no time in introducing himself to the professor. "Hi professor. Remember me? Jake Kimball. I was in your finance class at U of M, fall of 1970."

Rob shook hands and smiled as he searched his memory bank. So many students over a twenty-year teaching career. And now he had been retired from teaching for ten plus years.

"Hmmm. You say you were in my class at the University of Minnesota. That was actually my first teaching job. Wait a minute. Were you by chance the student who helped me get my car started after that first class? You had something you poured in the radiator to stop the leak. And then we used a bucket to get water and fill up the radiator."

Jake was smiling and nodding. "Yes, that was me. It was a good class, Finance 101, but as an Accounting major that was the only finance class I needed."

They continued talking as they walked out to the parking lot. Jake noticed they were heading in the direction of the Mercedes he had admired earlier. His first thought was serious doubt that a former college professor could own such an expensive car. Then he remembered Steve Peterson's comment in introducing Rob. Steve and Lori lived in one of the two penthouse suites on the top floor of one of the most expensive condos on the beach. And Steve had said that Rob lived on the same floor. All of this went through his mind as they continued to talk and were soon standing next to the Mercedes.

Jake's look of amazement was obvious. Rob smiled and said, "This is Old Betsy. A little different from the one you helped me with."

"Professor I don't mean to be nosey but I've got to ask. What did you do, win the lottery?"

"No Jake, not the lottery. But I guess you could say I discovered a money tree." Rob paused and seemed lost in thought for a moment. Then he noticed that Jake was waiting patiently for more information, like the good student he had been many years before.

"Jake it was right under my nose all those years I was teaching finance. About 15 years ago I discovered a way of earning a high rate of return on a stock portfolio with no additional risk. As soon as I knew for sure it was working I retired from teaching and devoted all my time to investing. Say Jake it's good to see you. I'll probably be joining the club." Rob pulled out his PDA, pushed a button and the powerful engine purred smoothly as the driver's side door swung open.

"But professor, wait. What did you mean by "money tree" and "high rate of return"? How can I learn more about this?" Jake hoped he didn't sound desperate.

"Hmmm. Maybe it is about time I became a professor again. Let me make a quick call."

"Hello Jean. I'm going to be about 30 minutes late. I met an old friend at the Rotary meeting. Yes love. I love you too. Meet at the same place, thirty minutes later." Then he reached in his car and retrieved a notebook. "I have an example in here. Let's go back inside and sit down at a table."

Tiffany, the hostess, greeted them with a warm smile and escorted them to a secluded table when they explained their purpose. "You won't be disturbed here," she said. "Can I bring you tea or coffee?"

Jake felt a sense of high anticipation. They waited for Tiffany to bring cups of herbal tea. Finally Rob pulled a single sheet of paper out of his notebook, looked at the paper and looked at Jake. Then he slid the single sheet of paper across the table.

2

Covered Calls

"A genius is a talented person who does his homework."
Thomas A. Edison

"Jake what I am about to show you is very simple and yet very powerful. I've only got time to give you a quick overview right now. I promise we will get together again. In fact if you are really interested I'll give you a homework assignment. Here, take a look at an investment I made in Network Associates. It's one of the top companies that provides virus detection software. If you use a PC their virus scanning software is most likely on your system."

The paper contained the following table:

NETWORK ASSOCIATES	NET	MAR	JUN	SEP	DEC
03-26-03 B	1000		14.90	14905.00	-14905.00
03-26-03 S	10 MAY 15.00		1.35	1324.96	-13580.04 CE
05-19-03 S	10 SEP 15.00		1.60	1574.92	-12005.12 CE
09-19-03 S	10 DEC 15.00		1.55	1529.92	-10475.20 CA
12-19-03 C	1000		15.00	14980.29	4505.09

Rob remained silent. After a couple of minutes Jake looked up.

"Professor, I believe I understand part of the first line. On March 26, 2003 you bought 1000 shares of Network Associates at $14.90 a share. But I'm not sure I understand the last two columns. Where did the 14905.00 come from? And why do the numbers in the last column go from negative to positive?"

7

"This is my short hand way of keeping up with my investments," explained Rob. "I have developed a software program that analyzes each of my investments as part of my overall portfolio. My primary concern is cash flow. I don't like to lose money. On each investment my first objective is to have a positive cash flow. My second objective is to have a *very* positive cash flow. But more about that later. First let's make sure you understand the basics here.

"You are correct that I bought 1000 shares of Network Associates. The price per share was $14.90. I use a discount, on-line broker and the sales commission was $5.00. Add the sales commission of $5.00 to the purchase of 1000 shares at $14.90 a share and you have my total cash outflow. For this one purchase my total cash outflow was $14,905.00. The next to the last column is the transaction amount and the last column is a running total or the cumulative effect of all the transactions. Since this was a cash outflow the dollar amount is shown as a negative.

"But now let's take a look at the second line of the Network Associates chart. On the same day that I bought the 1000 shares, I sold 10 contracts of May calls at a strike price of $15. The S in the first column means I made a sale. In the next column the "10 MAY 15.00" tells me what I sold. One contract is for 100 shares, the minimum needed to sell an option. So my 1000 shares of stock allow me to sell 10 contracts. That means that at the time the market price of Network Associates was $14.90 a share I sold the option for someone to buy my 1000 shares for $15 a share any time up until the close of the market on the third Friday the following May. $15 is the strike price. If the market price stays at or below $15 it will not be profitable for the buyer of the option to buy my shares for $15. Only if the market price goes above $15 will it be profitable for the option buyer to exercise the option. The price I received for that option was $1.35 per share. Less commission that came to $1,324.96.

"Notice that the transaction amount, next to last column, is positive. Selling the call means I received money so it is a cash inflow.

That has the effect of reducing the cumulative balance in the last column. At this point my net investment is $13,580.04 for the 1000 shares of Network Associates.

"My strategy here is called a covered call. That means I owned the stock, 1000 shares of Network Associates, and on those shares I sold a call option. It's called a "covered" call because, in the event the stock is called, I'm already covered. I already own the stock and can readily hand it over. The purchaser of the option has the right, but not the obligation, to purchase my 1000 shares of Network Associates for $15 a share anytime up to the close of the market on May 16, 2003. I received the premium of $1,324.96 for selling that right or option. Now the purchaser can be expected to exercise the option if the market price of Network Associates goes above $15 during that time period. It could be exercised anytime before expiration but most likely the option would not be exercised until the last day of the option period. Of course it would be foolish to exercise the option if the market price remains below $15.

"As it turned out the call option was not exercised. See the "CE" at the end of line two. CE stands for Call Expired."

Jake was beginning to see an entirely new concept in stock ownership. "Hmmm," he began, "you are actually generating a stream of income just from owning stocks. Do many people do this? I don't think I've heard about it before. I've got a lot of questions. Are there many stocks that you can do this with? What kind of investment return can you make?"

"Hold on Jake. First let me ask you a few questions. Maybe it would be best if you told me your impression of the stock market." Rob's professorial techniques were kicking in.

Jake and Katie had most of their funds invested in the stock market. They were in mutual funds managed by their investment advisor. Jake thought for a moment before responding.

"Individual stocks go up and down. Over time most of the stocks go up more than they go down so the overall market goes up gradually over time. The market is risky because some stocks go down more than up and may even end up worthless. We have our investments diversified in mutual funds to minimize the risks. That's about all I know. Well I guess I could add what my investment advisor says. His name is Nicholas Abbott. According to Nicholas your best strategy is to just sit tight for the long haul. Don't try to time the market. Don't worry about the ups and downs because over the long haul it will be up. And of course, his main advice, *trust Nicholas* to put us in decent mutual funds.

"As for options," Jake continued, "I've always heard of people buying options and that's a gamble that the stock will shoot up. If it does you make a lot of money. But I always thought of that as gambling, like playing blackjack in Vegas. It never occurred to me that people actually sell options."

Rob nodded. "That's a pretty good analysis of the market, Jake. And you are right, a lot of people buy stock options hoping the underlying stock will shoot up. But it is much more likely that the stock will move in a narrow range in a short period of time. My motto is *You make money by selling, not by buying.*

"Here's my pocket calculator and your first test for this semester. What was my return on investment from selling those ten contracts on March 26, 2003? By the way one contract is for 100 shares of stock."

Jake eagerly took the calculator and began solving the problem. He decided that the return for selling the call was $1,324.96. Now what should be the investment base to divide into the return? Well apparently the total cash outflow of $14,905.00. Dividing the former by the later he got 8.89%. He started to state the answer but then the thought occurred: over what time period. He smelled a trap. Sure, 8.89% was a good return but that was for less than a year. What was the APR, annual percentage rate? How many days from March 26, 2003 to May 19, 2003? A quick count gave him 54 days. So to annualize the return he multiplied 8.89% by 365 and divided by 54.

Looking at the professor he said, "60% sir."

"Very good Jake. Actually I never bother to annualize. I have another technique that I'll tell you about later. I'm satisfied with a good, quick return. Just for the heck of it why don't you compute the return for line three."

Jake quickly noted that the premium per share for the next sell of ten call contracts was $1.60 per share. After commissions Rob had netted $1,574.92. Now what was the amount of investment at that time? Presumably $13,580.04. He quickly made the computation.

"I get 11.59% without annualizing. However annualizing would be fairly simple. It took four months to earn the 11.59%. So just triple it for the APR. Either way it's a darn good return.

"I'm beginning to get the hang of this. The CE on the end of your net investment on line three means the call expired so you were able to do it again. I'll compute the gain on line four. Let's see. You again sold 10 contacts, this time at $1.55 per share. After commissions you netted $1,529.92. By the way Professor when do you get this money?"

"It goes immediately into my brokerage account. I can take it out and spend it or I can invest it. The choice is mine. I earned it by selling the option."

Jake was amazed as the concept sunk in. "So this really is *new money*. You have earned money on your portfolio but it's not capital gains and it's not dividends. I had no idea you could do this."

Rob smiled. He always enjoyed seeing the light come on with his students as he explained a new financial concept.

"Very good. Now here's another question for you. Most investment advisors say the way to make money in the stock market is to buy good stocks and hold for long-term appreciation. That's apparently the plan your investment advisor is following. How much of my return on Network Associates was a result of stock appreciation or dividends?"

Jake knew better than to make a snap response. He looked closely at the chart again.

"Professor you told me that CE stands for Call Expired. What does CA stand for?"

"CA stands for Call Assigned. Notice the last column of line four is -10475.20CA. That means that on December 19, 2003 the market price of Network Associates was above $15 a share and the owners of the call option exercised their rights. They bought my 1000 shares for $15 a share. My 1000 shares were assigned to the option holders. That's shown in line five where I have a C for Called in the first column after the date, 12-19-03. On that date the shares were called which means I sold them for the strike price, $15. You can see by the balance in the last column that my profit for this investment was $4,505.09. So now you should be able to tell me how much of that profit was from stock appreciation or dividends."

NETWORK ASSOCIATES		NET	MAR	JUN	SEP	DEC
03-26-03 B	1000		14.90	14905.00	-14905.00	
03-26-03 S	10 MAY 15.00		1.35	1324.96	-13580.04 CE	
05-19-03 S	10 SEP 15.00		1.60	1574.92	-12005.12 CE	
09-19-03 S	10 DEC 15.00		1.55	1529.92	-10475.20 CA	
12-19-03 C	1000		15.00	14980.29	4505.09	

Jake thought for another moment as he analyzed the chart. Finally he said, "You bought the 1000 shares for $14.90 each and sold them for $15 each. That's a ten cent per share gain. But that was really a small part of your over all gain. Almost all of your return was from selling the call options. Apparently none of your return was from dividends. I would say you made 10 cents a share, or $100, from stock appreciation. And the rest, $4400 in less than nine months was from selling the options."

"That's right," said Rob. "I think of it as picking money from a money tree like you would pick fruit from, say, an orange tree. I tend to do short term option sales, pick some dollars and hope to get called. I don't mind if the stock shoots up and the option buyer makes a big profit. Usually the option expires and I can pick some more fruit from the same tree. In this example I picked dollars three times from the little money tree. I'm happy with a good return every few months."

As the professor began to gather his papers Jake was thinking fast.

"But wait a minute," Jake exclaimed. "There has got to be a catch. This is too good to be true. What if you are picking fruit as the price of the stock is headed down?"

"Good point. And it can happen. In fact I think I have another example here that illustrates just that experience." Rob pulled a sheet of paper out of his note book and handed it to Jake.

"Cott Corporation is a soft drink bottler. You can see that its stock price went from $9.50 a share down to $3.81 a share. During that time I picked so much fruit from the tree I made a profit of $9,847.80 even though I finally sold the stock at a loss.

"There is a definite risk in owning stock," Rob continued. "But that risk can be greatly mitigated, and in some cases even overcome, by selling calls. This particular investment reminds me of a small town in Minnesota. Have you ever heard of the town of Andover?"

Jake's head was reeling as he was still analyzing the sheet of paper detailing Rob's investment in Cott. He was counting the number of times calls had been sold on this one investment. He just managed to look up and mumble, "No, don't think so."

"The story of how the town got its name is interesting. The Great

COTT CORPORATION COTT		FEB	MAY	AUG	NOV
11-08-94 B	1500	9.5000	14279.00		-14279.00
11-08-94 S	15 MAY 10.000	1.5625	2298.67		-11980.33 CE
11-30-94 B	1500	10.000	15029.00		-27009.33
11-30-94 S	15 MAY 10.00	1.7500	2579.91		-24429.42 CE
02-09-95 B	2000	9.625	19279.00		-43708.42
02-09-95 S	20 AUG 10.00	1.3750	2694.90		-41013.52 CE
05-22-95 S	30 NOV 10.000	.9375	2742.40		-38271.12 CE
08-22-95 S	20 NOV 10.000	.6250	1199.95		-37071.17 CE
11-15-95 S	50 MAY 10.000	.6250	3024.89		-34046.28 CE
05-20-96 S	50 NOV 10.000	.7500	3649.87		-30396.41 CE
11-18-96 S	50 MAY 10.000	.4375	2087.42		-28308.99 CE
05-19-97 S	50 AUG 10.000	.6250	3024.89		-25284.10 CE
08-18-97 S	20 NOV 10.000	.6250	1199.95		-24084.15 CE
08-18-97 S	30 NOV 10.000	.5625	1637.44		-22446.71 CE
11-24-97 S	50 FEB 10.000	.7500	3649.87		-18796.84 CE
02-24-98 S	50 MAY 10.000	.6250	3024.89		-15771.95 CE
05-15-98 S	50 AUG 7.500	.5000	2397.41		-13374.54 CE
08-25-98 S	50 NOV 7.500	.5000	2397.41		-10977.13 CE
11-17-98 S	50 MAY 7.500	.3750	1772.43		-9204.70 CE
06-23-99 S	5000	.8120	19052.50		9847.80

Northern Railroad had a stop at a small northern town in the late nineteen twenties. One morning there was a derailment and the train rolled over and over and over. This accident was such a big news story the residents decided to change the town name to Andover, to capture the event forever in history. I'm reminded of the name, Andover, when I sell calls over and over."

Jake was still full of questions as Rob's PDA rang. "Yes Jean. I'm on the way. I'll see you in 10 minutes."

Looking at Jake he said, "Good thing this is a small island. OK you've learned a lot. Now here's your homework assignment. Get a copy of the Wall Street Journal or Investors Business Daily. Go to the options page and pick three stocks that you are familiar with. I want you to assume a purchase of 100 shares of stock and sale of one covered call contract. Pick an option where the strike price—that is the price for which you are committed to sell—is close to the market price. Don't worry this will all become clear when you do the exercise. Remember once you've bought the stock you have assumed the risk of stock ownership. What you are doing by selling calls is generating income, *picking dollars off the money tree.* You should be taking notes by the way.

"Here's a sheet of paper. Let's start over. First go to the options page. Your local paper may also have an options page. You might find prices for both calls and puts. For now just concentrate on calls. Pick three stocks. Now for each stock pick four different call option contracts. The four options on each stock will differ by strike price or expiration date. Notice how the first Networks Associates option I sold was designated. It reads 10 May 15.00. That means the strike price is $15 for the 10 contracts. Options expire on the third Friday of each month. Since this a May option in 2003 the expiration date is May 16. I suggest you select for analysis four different call option contracts for each stock.

"Using Network Associates again as an example, I sold May 15. Others that I considered were May 17.50, June 15.00, and June 17.50. Do you see what I am saying? On that one stock I considered four different possible option sales. Look at options from the standpoint both of strike price and expiration date. Since we are considering two strike prices and two expiration dates we have four possible combinations. Now compute the return for each of the four contracts assuming first CE and then CA. Those are the only two things that can happen. Either the call will expire, CE, or the call will be assigned, CA. Compute your return both ways. You will be making a total of 12 computations, four for each of the three stocks.

"You might as well write down the formulas for computing the return. They are:

$$\text{If Sold} = \frac{(\text{Strike Price} + \text{Premium} - \text{Purchase Price})}{\text{Purchase Price}}$$

$$\text{If Expired} = \frac{\text{Premium}}{\text{Purchase Price}}$$

"You'll be surprised how much you learn just doing this exercise."

Jake was writing furiously on the sheet of paper. He looked up to see the professor headed for the door.

"Professor, I've got questions. And when will you check my homework?"

Rob's PDA rang before he got to the door. Pulling out the phone and looking over his shoulder at Jake he said, "I'll come back to Rotary next week. See you then."

And he was gone.

3

Take Control

"Failure is the opportunity to begin again, more intelligently."
Henry Ford

"Katie my love, you are not going to believe who I met at Rotary today." Jake arrived home in a state of excitement with his newly purchased copy of the Wall Street Journal.

"Let me guess," replied Katie with a sly smile. "Could it possibly have been Rob Graham, the Finance Professor you had in college?" As Jake's mouth hung open she continued. "I've just been on the phone with Lori. Steve is rather perturbed with you. He says you shanghaied his guest before he could introduce him to the membership chair and the president. According to Lori the only way we can make up for your outrageous indiscretion is for us to come over for cocktails and sunset on their balcony. So I accepted. Is that alright?"

"Sure. You know I'm always glad to visit with Steve and Lori. Besides I need to pick Steve's brain. He retired near the top of that big brokerage firm. With all the money they have he must have done really well as a stockbroker, or analyst, whatever he was. But right now I've got homework to do. I'm computing how much money we can make by selling covered calls."

"Covered who? Oh never mind. Just let me know when I can read another chapter of your novel. I'm anxious to find out how your Walter Mitty CPA character saves the nation from financial ruin."

As Jake did his computations he became increasingly familiar with the operations of the options market. Several points became obvious. Apparently there were three factors in his decision process which determined the amount of premium he could receive by selling a call option.

First, the time period to the expiration date was important. The premium offered for one month was not as great as the premium offered for three months or six months. The longer the option was in effect the more it was worth. He also noticed the "time value" of money come into play. A six month option, while more than a three month option, was less than twice the value; a three month option, worth more than a one month option, was less than three times the value.

The second factor under his control was the selection of the strike price. If a stock were selling for $12.50, a strike price of $15 would pay less than a strike price of $10. That made sense because with a $15 strike price the stock would have to rise more than $2.50 before the option would be exercised. A strike price of $10 meant the stock was already $2.50 above the price at which it could be bought by the option holder. A strike price of $10 meant the option already had $2.50 of intrinsic value in addition to its time value.

The third factor was the particular stock that he selected. Jake found two stocks that had the same closing price the previous day. When he checked the option premium for each, using the same strike price and expiration date, he found that stock A would yield a significantly higher premium than stock B. Maybe that had something to do with the volatility of the stock. That would bear checking out.

He began to formulate some questions for the professor. First how do you know which stocks to buy? Is it just random or is there a way to wisely select stocks? Second how do you know which strike price and time period to choose? He began to suspect that once he had those questions answered there would be more questions. Also what was the deal with puts? He noticed that the stocks had both put and call options. He was deep in thought when Katie came over and pulled on his ear lobe.

"Let's go for a walk, handsome, and you can tell me how much money we are going to make with that covered stuff. We'll need to get back in plenty of time to make sunset with Steve and Lori."

*****

"Jake, I'll bet you were surprised to see Rob. I had no idea you two knew each other." Jake and Katie had enjoyed a vigorous walk on the beach, showered and changed before going to the Peterson's penthouse condo for sunset and cocktails. Steve was in a bombastic mood. He had already extolled the virtues of his favorite sports teams and denigrated the lack of virtue of certain local political figures.

"Yes," Jake replied. "I was very pleasantly surprised. Rob Graham was my Finance Professor over thirty years ago. He had a certain presence in the classroom, you might say charisma, that makes him easy to remember."

"You'll notice," Steve interrupted because this was his favorite time of day, "that the bottom of the sun has just touched the Gulf of Mexico. It will be exactly two minutes and forty six seconds until the sun is completely down. And I would say the conditions are good for a green flash this evening. Humidity is low and there are only a few clouds near the horizon."

The green flash was a popular topic of conversation. It occurred rarely and would only happen when the last of the sun dipped into the sea. Perhaps one time in a hundred a green flash could be seen just at that moment of last sunlight. You could consider yourself lucky if you saw it once. But of course the Petersons had seen it numerous times with their front row seat.

"Speaking of green," Jake piped in, "what do you think of making money in the options market?"

"You will lose your shirt," Steve replied with conviction. "You might as well go to Vegas and play the crap table. In my thirty years on Wall Street I never knew anyone to consistently make money buying options. It's just a gamble."

"Steve, I never did understand exactly what you did on Wall Street."

"I started off as a broker. And then I managed one of our branch offices with about 50 brokers. So we were basically in sales. I would have clients occasionally who would insist on playing the options market. After they lost all they could afford I would then get them into some good solid companies for long term growth. I tell you, people who think they can manage their own money in the stock market, why that's like trying to operate on yourself. There are some things that just need to be handled by professionals and the stock market is one of them. My clients over the years would just turn every thing over to me. They didn't want to be bothered with the decisions. And of course my job was to preserve their capital. I guess you could say my motto was 'preserve and grow slowly'. And it paid off. We've been retired for fifteen years now, enjoying the good life.

"You know the old 80-20 rule. It's formally called the Pareto Principle after the Italian economist who discovered that generally 80% of the wealth was owned by 20% of the people. But it applies to a lot more than just wealth distribution. For example 80% of my problems came from the 20% of my clients who were always coming up with a hot stock tip or strategy, like the ones who wanted to gamble in the options market. I would give those clients to new trainees and keep the satisfied clients. All brokers like clients who appreciate their knowledge and expertise. Leave the driving to us, so to speak."

Steve leaned back in the lounge chair and smiled contentedly, enjoying the warm breeze, commanding view of the beach and the gulf. Four pelicans gracefully flew by. There were sailboats in the distance. The clouds were just right to pick up a red tint from the sun.

"But what if, Steve, instead of buying options, you sold options.

And suppose further that you only sold options on stock that you already owned. Would that not be risk free income?"

Steve was about to take a sip of his margarita, Lori's specialty. Lori liked to brag that she had learned the secret recipe after chatting with the bartender at a local Mexican restaurant. The glass had reached Steve's lips and seemed to be frozen there. Time stood still. Finally Steve set the glass down and absent-mindedly licked the salt off his lips. His voice was usually a little on the loud side. But now it was low, just barely audible. He seemed almost to be talking to himself. "Hmmm. Sell options on stock that you own. Yes that would seem to work. Maybe that's why so many people buying options lose money. It's because people selling options are making money. If the stock goes up above the strike price you sell at a profit. You get the premium and part of the stock appreciation. If the stock goes down you still keep the premium. Psychologically you are not that concerned that the stock go up right away. Long term sure you want it to go up and, if you pick a good stock, it will. But if the stock goes down you could buy the option back for pennies on the dollar and sell it again when the stock goes back up. Or just wait for the option to expire and then sell a new contract on the same stock. What's the risk? Well the stock price could move up sharply and your gain on the up side would be limited. But that rarely happens. Stocks move up over time but over short periods like three months, they mostly just move up and down within a narrow range. Of course the real risk is that the stock could go down. But you have that risk whether you sell options or not. So if you mean by 'risk free income' no additional risk then . . ."

Steve interrupted his rambling monologue and shouted to Lori, "Honey, would you bring me the Wall Street Journal." And then to Jake, "I wonder what kind of premium I could get on my portfolio? Why you know the more I think about it the more obvious it is. Hardly any stocks pay a decent dividend any more. The portfolio is just sitting there. And I'm sitting here hoping the market will go up a little bit. I've got dozens of stocks that have been

virtually flat over the past couple of years. Might as well generate a little income while they're sitting there. Jake let me fix you
another drink. Lori, did you throw out the papers?"

Jake noticed that the sky had become even more beautiful after
the sunset. He smiled, looking forward to his next meeting with
the professor.

4

You Make Money by Selling— Not by Buying

"The hardest struggle of all is to be something different
from what the average man is."
Charles M. Schwab

Tiffany smiled when she saw Rob and Jake headed her way. "What are you guys doing here today? Rotary's not until Thursday." Tiffany had run on the college track team with Jake's daughter and fell in love with Marco Island while visiting on spring break. She and Jake were good friends and always kidded each other.

"Urgent business," Jake responded. "I'm learning how to plant a money tree. And if you give us good service I may show you how to plant one too." At Jake's request Rob had agreed to meet on Monday afternoon for a spot of tea and another investment lesson.

Tiffany seated them at a secluded table and went for the tea. Jake opened a folder in which he had his homework assignment and a series of questions.

"Professor, I hardly know where to start. Over the past 30 years I've generally invested any surplus funds in the market. But it's always been a straight investment and I generally just relied on the advice of my stock broker or a hot tip I got from a client. And I had a mutual fund IRA that I made regular contributions to. But after our discussion last week and the homework assignment I see a whole new possibility for earning income on a portfolio. I guess my key question is how to select stocks. Is it just random or is there a way to improve the odds. And also while I now have

23

some understanding of selling calls I don't have a clue about puts. Are puts part of the money tree. And there's the matter of...."

"Jake hold on." Rob grinned as Tiffany poured hot water on the herbal tea bag in each cup. "One step at a time."

Tiffany patted Jake on his head with slightly graying hair which made him look dignified and said, "I overheard part of what you two were talking about last week." Turning to Rob and holding out her hand she said, "By the way, I'm Tiffany. Welcome to Marco Island."

"Thank you Tiffany. The hospitality is great and the weather is terrific. Are you interested in investments?"

"Oh yes. I joined an investment club. We're members of NAIC. There are 20 of us pooling $50 a week. So far at our meetings no one has mentioned options. I wonder if you would be willing to make a presentation."

Just then two couples entered the restaurant. "Got to go. I'll be back," as she bustled off.

"She's a great kid," Jake commented. "And a real hustler. I've never seen a young person with such eclectic interests. She writes articles for the local paper, coaches young girls at the Y in volleyball and basketball and frequently is in plays produced by Marco Players our community theater group. And now, by golly, she's interested in investments."

"But professor," Jake continued. "Where do we go from here? I want to learn it all. But I know what you said is important. 'One step at a time'."

"I've given that some thought," Rob began. "Here's the order in which we should proceed:

"First, we should complete what I call *the money tree concept*. This is the process of selling—with emphasis on selling, not buying—options, both calls and puts. Last week we talked about calls. Today I will explain puts. Even though you will soon understand calls and puts, you will not be ready to execute a trade until you have fully mastered the next three lessons.

"Second, we need to build a prospect list of stocks. The key here is which stocks you allow onto your prospect list. Not all stocks are equal. I have developed definite criteria. Not complicated, just five basic tests that a stock must pass before it is allowed on my list. Those five tests protected me from the recent debacle known as the internet bubble.

"Third, once the prospect list is in place we need to rank the stocks on the list before deciding on an investment. I have developed two formulas for this. One is the Buy Limit which tells us the maximum price that you would pay for a stock. And the second is the Buy Rank which ranks the stocks based on their relative attractiveness. The formulas are not really complicated but it can get cumbersome if you are dealing with say 50 or 100 stocks on the prospect list. So I have developed a software program that will allow you to sort your list, based on Buy Rank, or any other criteria, with just a few key strokes.

"Fourth, and finally, we come to execution. There are specific steps as well as record keeping I recommend in executing the order."

Rob paused for a sip of tea. It had gotten cool. As if reading his mind Tiffany appeared with fresh hot cups for both of them.

Jake was taking notes. Two competing thoughts were going through his mind: *Why didn't I know about this sooner?* And *Perhaps I can become master of my own investments!*

"I'm ready," he said hoping it didn't sound like a plea. "Let's take the next step."

Rob slid a chart across the table and turned it so Jake could read it.

"Calls and puts can be bought and sold," Rob explained. "That gives four possible transactions. There are many exotic strategies that make use of various combinations of these four basic transactions. I've examined and used most if not all of them. From my experience your best results will come from the right side of the chart. Remember my motto: *You make money by selling not by buying.*

CALLS			
	Buy a Call You have the right to purchase a stock at a specified price for a certain period of time.	**Write (sell) a Call** You have an obligation to sell a stock at a specified price for a certain period of time, if the buyer activates the Call.	
BUY	**Buy a Put** You have the right to sell a stock at a specified price for a certain period of time.	**Write (sell) a Put** You have a obligation to buy a stock at a specified price for a certain period of time, if the buyer activates the Put	**SELL**
PUTS			

"Selling a put option means you incur the same risk as owning the stock on which you sell the put. Typically you will sell a put with a strike price less than the current price of the stock. If the stock goes down you are obligated to buy it at the strike price which may be higher than the current stock price. If the stock goes up or remains about the same during the option period, the put will expire.

"What the buyer of the put option gets is the right to sell you that stock at the strike price until the option period expires. Investors buying puts are buying insurance against the possibility that the stock will take a dive. You on the other hand, the seller of the put, have done your homework on the stock and are reasonably confidant it is going up. We'll get into stock selection later.

"Are you with me so far?"

Jake had been listening carefully and taking notes. "Yes I think so. One thing I like about the covered calls is that in a sense it is risk free. Of course owning stock is not risk free. It can always go down and you have a loss. But there is no additional risk associated with the call option. Either the option will expire or you will sell the stock at a price you have agreed to. But that doesn't seem to be the case with puts."

"That's right," Rob agreed. "At least that's the way I do it. Some people sell call options naked, that is without owning the stock. There is tremendous risk in that strategy. If the stock shoots up in price you could be forced to pay that high price for the stock and then immediately sell it at the lower strike price to comply with the option you sold. Naked calls are very risky. There's no limit to how high the stock could go, even if only temporarily, and create for you a tremendous loss. I always sell covered calls and never naked calls.

"Now with puts it's a little different. A covered put means selling a put on a stock that you have already sold short at the same strike price. So if you are forced to buy the stock you are just closing your short position. The money you earned by selling the put is eaten up by the transaction of selling the stock short and then buying it back. And of course if the stock goes up the put option expires but you lose money on the short sell of the stock. The higher the stock goes the more you lose. Covered puts are not appealing to me. Perhaps I'm just an optimistic bull and like to design a strategy based on the market going up.

"So in the case of puts I sell naked puts. There is risk of course. But at least the risk is limited in that the stock can not go below zero. That's not true of a naked call. The way I look at a naked put is this. Either the stock will go up and the option expires or the stock goes down and I get to buy a desired stock at a discount. If the later happens I analyze the stock again to make sure it is still desirable and then sell a covered call."

Jake was taking notes and scratching his head at the same time. "Professor I think I need a picture."

"OK. Take a look at this transaction. It's one of my typical naked puts."

Rob again slid a single sheet of paper across the table.

5

The Naked Put

*"A man without financial surplus is controlled by circumstances,
whereas a man with financial surplus controls his circumstances."*
Harvey Firestone

CITRIX SYSTEMS	CTXS	MAR	JUN	SEP	DEC
06-13-00 S	20 DEC 20.00	4.875	9699.66		9699.66 PE
06-14-00 S	20 SEP 20.00	2.500	4949.92		14649.48 PE
06-20-00 S	20 DEC 17.50	2.750	5449.81		20099.29 PE
06-26-00 S	20 DEC 17.50	3.250	6449.78		26549.07 PE
06-26-00 S	20 DEC 15.00	2.062	4074.86		30623.93 PE
08-14-00 S	20 SEP 17.50	1.000	1949.93		32573.86 PE
08-28-00 S	20 MAR 17.50	2.750	5449.81		38023.67 PE
09-25-00 S	20 MAR 15.00	1.812	3574.87		41598.54 PE

After a few moments Rob said, "Sometimes you get lucky and never have the naked puts assigned. Here is such an example with Citrix Systems. Citrix Systems is a supplier of applications server software and services. Tell me what you see."

Jake had been studying the chart intently for several minutes. "This may be too good to be true. There's got to be a catch here somewhere. What am I missing?"

"Well," Jake continued, "I remember from the covered call chart on Network Associates that each line represents a transaction. So on June 13, 2000 you sold puts on 20 contracts, 2000 shares, of CTXS. DEC 20 means the option will expire or be exercised on the third Friday in December. If the stock price is below $20 the holder of the option will require you to buy his 2000 shares for $20. If the stock price is above $20 the option will expire, which is apparently what happened. PE must stand for put expired. In exchange for selling that option you received $4.875 per share or $9699.66 net of commission. You continued doing that, selling naked puts on CTXS, and over a nine month period, June to the following March, earned $41,598.54. How did I do?"

"Excellent! Later I will explain how CTXS worked its way to the top of my prospect list. I wouldn't have made these transactions on just any stock. But for now let's focus on the naked put as part of the money tree concept.

"Again it is very different from the traditional buy and hold strategy. In fact with naked puts I may never own the stock. Of course it has to be a stock that I would be willing to own because the put might be assigned. But again the concept is to take short term gains on a continuous basis on stocks that I own (covered calls) or stocks that I would be willing to own (naked puts). I pick some fruit off the tree and move on. There are always more trees with more fruit.

"Notice on CTXS that the first premium of $4.875 represents a discount of 24.3% to the $20 strike, six months out, if it had been assigned. On the following day I sold 20 more contracts at $2.50 per share. This would provide a 12.5% discount to the $20 strike, three months out, if it had been assigned. Twice the discount for twice the time period. "

"I see," Jake exclaimed. *"Time is money!* So, What is the desired premium for a naked put?"

"My goal on naked puts is to get at least 10% discount in the shortest time frame. An exception to the rule was the transaction on August 14. The stock closed that day at $20.69. I received only a $1.00 premium for a $17.50 strike price but the time frame was just a little over a month.

"Here is a guideline when considering naked put opportunities. The elements that may affect the possible outcome are:

    1) the strike month (time to expiration),

    2) the put option premium and resultant discount to strike price, and

    3) the current stock price.

"As you have noticed the farther you go out in time the higher the put option premium and therefore the larger the discount. This discount is also dependent on the strike price in relation to the current stock price. The bigger the difference between the current stock price and the strike price the lower the premium. We want to combine these three factors in a way that provides good opportunities but also guides us away from doing the wrong thing. With this in mind use the following to calculate a Put Factor for your prospects.

$$\text{Put Factor} \;=\; \frac{6\,(100\ \text{PR})\,(\text{CP} - \text{SP})}{(\text{ME})\,(\text{SP})\,(\text{SP})}$$

Where:

ME = Months to Expiration

PR = Put Option Premium

CP = Current Stock Price

SP = Strike Price

"I have had excellent success with naked puts for stocks when this factor is greater than one. Let's use my Put Option Wizard to calculate the factor for the first trade.

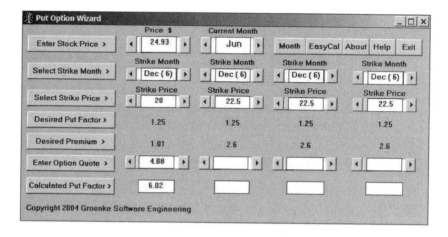

"Here is a summary for all the trades.

Put Factors for CTXS					
Date	Stock Price	Put Option Month and Strike Price	Put Option Premium	Months to Expiration	Put Factor
6/13/2000	24.93	Dec 20.00	4.88	6	6.02
6/14/2000	23.88	Sep 20.00	2.50	3	4.85
6/20/2000	20.44	Dec 17.50	2.75	6	2.65
6/26/2000	19.50	Dec 17.50	3.25	6	2.13
6/26/2000	19.50	Dec 15.00	2.06	6	4.13
8/14/2000	20.69	Sep 17.50	1.00	1	6.25
8/28/2000	22.56	Mar 17.50	2.75	7	3.90
9/25/2000	18.31	Mar 15.00	1.81	6	2.67

"Be very cautious if this factor is less than one. If it is negative you have selected a strike price that is greater than the current stock price. Make sure this is what you want to do since your chances of assignment are much greater but still at a discount.

"You mentioned there must be a catch. There is an investment needed to accomplish a naked put trade even though it is not shown on the chart. Since these are naked puts you need sufficient cash or margin in your brokerage account to make these trades. The amount varies by brokerage firm. I did these options with Brown & Company. Their requirement is a cash or margin reserve of 20% of the put purchase price plus the premiums received. If this is a cash reserve it is earning interest at the broker margin rate so in a sense one could be double dipping—earning premiums and interest!

"Let's say you like a certain stock and would like to invest in it over time. But you are a little concerned about current trend and momentum. I use a strategy I call *Double Up*. I buy 50% of the desired investment now and sell a covered call with strike price close to or a little above market price. I also sell an equal number of naked puts at a strike price lower than the current market price. My Double Up strategy has three possible results:

"**Stock Price Down** in which case the puts are assigned and the calls will expire. I now have my intended investment and continue to sell covered calls.

"**Stock Price Close To Unchanged** in which case the puts and calls expire and I repeat the process, selling covered calls and naked puts, picking more money off the money tree.

"**Stock Price Up** in which case the calls are assigned, the puts expire, and I am back to a total cash position with respect to this investment with a significant gain. I can decide if I should reinvest in this stock, Double Up again, or move on to another stock on my prospect list.

"Here's an example that illustrates my Double Up strategy. The company is Lockheed Martin (LMT), one of the largest defense contractors in North America. They had just received large contracts for new fighters from the Defense Department when I started this sequence."

Rob slid the Lockheed-Martin chart across the table.

LOCKHEED-MARTIN	LMT	MAR	JUN	SEP	DEC
01-03-00 B	2000	22.1875	44385.00	-44385.00	
01-03-00 S	20 JUN 22.50	3.000	5949.80	-38435.20 CA	
01-05-00 S	20 MAR 20.00	1.6875	3324.88	-35110.32 PA	
03-08-00 S	50 SEP 17.50	2.3125	11459.61	-23650.71 PE	
03-17-00 S	30 SEP 17.50	2.250	6682.27	-16968.44 PE	
03-17-00 B	2000	20.00	40019.00	-56987.44	
03-20-00 S	20 SEP 20.00	2.0625	4074.86	-52912.58 CA	
06-16-00 C	2000	22.50	44979.50	-7933.08	
08-30-00 C	1500	20.00	29980.00	22046.92	
09-15-00 C	500	20.00	9980.66	32027.58	

"I decided that an investment of 4000 shares would be in order. So using my Double Up strategy on January 3, I bought 2000 shares at $22.18 and sold June calls with a $22.50 strike price. I earned $5,949.80 on the transaction. Two days later I sold 20 contracts of March puts with a strike price of $20 earning an additional $3,324.88. In early March I determined that I would probably be assigned the puts. I also decided the stock would not go much lower and was ready for an upswing. So I sold first 50 contracts of September puts at a $17.50 strike price and then another 30 contracts at the same. I earned over $18,000 on those two transactions. Sure enough the 20 March 20 call contracts that I sold on January 5 were assigned to me, meaning I bought an additional 2000 shares at $20. I sold calls on those 2000 share earning $4,074.86.

"As I had expected the stock continued moving up. The 4000 shares on which I had sold calls were purchased for $20 and the put contracts I had sold expired. As of September 15 I was in an all cash position with respect to LMT. I had earned $32,027.58 over a nine month period. My average investment was approximately $31,000 which provided a nine month gain of 103.3%.

"As it happened LMT continued to rise in price and eventually after several years doubled. I could have bought and held 4000 shares in the traditional manner and after about three years I would have done as well as I accomplished with the money tree strategy in nine months. The money tree strategy is both quicker and not dependent on a sharp increase in stock price.

"So Jake, would you like to see a few more examples of Double Up?

"Here are two software companies," Rob said as he looked through his folder. "They demonstrate how you can improve the return on a covered call strategy by selling a naked put also. The first is BEA Systems."

"Jake you should be pretty good at reading these charts now."

"Yes I think so. You bought 1000 shares, sold a covered call and then two naked puts all at a $10 strike price. Apparently the stock price was above $10 on the expiration dates because the call was assigned, CA, and both puts expired, PE. You ended with all cash. A nifty little profit of $3,225.34."

BEA SYSTEMS	BEAS	JAN	APR	JUL	OCT
04-21-03 B	1000	10.40	10410.00	-10410.00	
04-21-03 S	10 JUN 10.00	1.25	1224.94	-9185.06 CA	
04-28-03 S	10 SEP 10.00	1.15	1124.94	-8060.12 PE	
05-12-03 S	10 MAY 10.00	.20	174.99	-7885.13 PE	
06-20-03 C	1000	10.00	9980.53	2095.40	
07-03-03 S	10 DEC 10.00	1.15	1129.94	3225.34 PE	

"Right, and it's interesting to me if you break down the profit into two parts," Rob replied. "If I had done only covered calls the profit would have been $1224.94 or 11.76%. Decent enough but the puts boosted the profit to $3225.34, a percentage gain of 30.98%.

"Here's another similar investment, another software company."

"Again my profits were enhanced by adding puts to the basic covered call strategy.

COMPUWARE CORP	CPWR	FEB	MAY	AUG	NOV
05-07-03 B	2000	4.91	9810.00	-9810.00	
05-07-03 S	20 NOV 5.00	.55	1059.96	-8750.04 CA	
05-07-03 S	20 NOV 5.00	.95	1859.89	-6890.15 PE	
05-16-03 S	10 JUN 5.00	.30	274.98	-6615.17 PE	
11-21-03 C	2000	5.00	9980.53	3365.36	

"There is one more variation that I use. Before I get to that Jake, would you summarize what we've covered so far?"

"Sure," Jake replied looking quickly at his notes. "We started off with . . . I guess you would call it a pure naked put. Citrix Systems. You sold numerous puts and they all expired. By the way how would you compute your return on that?"

Rob smiled, shrugged his shoulders and said, "Some say infinity since the investment was zero. Or is it to infinity and beyond?"

Jake looked over his notes again and continued. "So the first one is the pure naked put where all your puts expire and you never actually own the stock. And the second one is the Double Up where you buy half of your intended investment and sell puts for the other half. And you say there is one more. Hmmm. Could it be a case where you intend to have a pure naked put but you have to buy the stock?"

"Very good," Rob congratulated his former and now once again student. "Always, when I sell a put, it is on a stock that I would not mind buying, especially at the discounted strike price. So I know that's a possibility. And since it is a stock I am willing to buy it is one I am willing to sell a covered call on. Here are a couple of examples of my Put to Covered Call Strategy."

MICRON TECHNOLOGY	MU	JAN	APR	JU	OCT
01-15-03 S	10 FEB 10.00	.85	824.97		824.97 PA
02-21-03 B	1000	10.00	10019.00		-9194.03
02-24-03 S	10 JUL 10.00	.60	584.98		-8609.05 CA
02-24-03 S	10 JUL 7.50	1.40	1374.95		-7234.10 PE
07-18-03 C	1000	10.00	9980.83		2746.73

"On January 15 my analysis indicated that Micron Technology had hit its low point and would be moving up. I sold a naked put, 10 contracts one month out. I was almost right. The price dipped below $10 just in time for me to have the put assigned. I sold a covered call on the 1000 shares I was required to buy and also sold another naked put. The stock proceeded up and I was back in an all cash position.

"Now here's the final example I have with me.

TEXAS INSTRUMENT	TXN	JAN	APR	JUL	OCT
06-05-03 S	10 JUN 20.00	.45	429.97		429.97 PA
06-20-03 B	1000	20.00	20019.00	-19589.03	
06-20-03 S	10 JUL 20.00	.40	374.98	-19214.05 CE	
07-03-03 S	10 AUG 17.50	.75	729.96	-18484.09 PE	
07-21-03 S	10 OCT 20.00	.75	729.96	-17754.13 CA	
10-17-03 C	1000	20.00	19980.00	2225.87	

"Again I started off with a pure naked put strategy. When the stock was assigned to me because the price dipped below $20 I converted to the covered call strategy aided by an additional naked put."

"Any guidelines on what level of put activity one should commit to?" Jake asked.

"Limit yourself to 20% or less of your account value that you have tied up supporting naked puts. Look at this as a way to preplan some of your new investments for some of your covered calls which may be assigned. You might as well buy stocks at a discount if you can."

"One could also sell only naked puts against an all cash account. The strategy here is you would only begin to own any stocks through the assignment of a put. All of your stock purchases are then at a discount. Again you would only do this with companies you would like to own but at a lower price."

"Okay professor I'm ready. I can't wait to get started. This seems too good to be true but what can be the catch."

Rob smiled as he looked at his student and thought to himself, *my friend you are not even close to being ready.* To Jake he said, "Actually there is a catch."

Jake's face dropped. "But professor you've shown me it works and you've made a fortune with the money tree strategy. What do you mean about a catch?

"Jake, suppose you were ready to get started, what is the first thing you would do?"

"I guess I would start off slow with just the covered call strategy. I would learn that first before going to naked puts. Right?"

"Right," Rob agreed. "And what is the first thing you would need to do?"

"Buy a stock."

"Which stock?"

After a moment...."Oh," Jake nodded in agreement. "Which stock. Which stock indeed!"

"We've still got much work to do. Thursday after Rotary I will begin explaining my stock selection strategy."

"I'll get the bill," said Jake.

"Let's not forget a good tip for Tiffany."

6

Build the Prospect List

"Apply yourself; get all the education you can, but then…
do something. Don't just stand there, make it happen."
Lee Iacocca

The Rotary Club meeting had ended and Jake had waited patiently as Rob met the Membership Chairman and filled out the paperwork to be proposed for membership. Tiffany had again seated them at a secluded table and brought each a cup of herbal tea.

Rob noticed how diligently Jake was going over his notes as he waited and commented, "I seem to recall that you made an A in my Finance 101 course."

Jake laughed. "No not exactly professor. I had an A going into the final. But then I got distracted toward the end of the semester. Her name is Katie. I would like for you to meet her. We've been blessed with three daughters and five grandkids."

"That's wonderful. Jean and I enjoy our kids and grandkids too. But let's get back to business. I've got two questions for you. First, do you understand the money tree concept?"

"I think so," Jake responded as he gathered his thoughts. "To me it's a rather radical concept for investing. Different from all my traditional understanding. We had a speaker at the Forum Club in Naples recently. A guy named John Bogle. He made a lot of sense. His strategy seems to be to invest in an index fund, keep transaction costs low and ride the market up over the long term. Last week Katie and I had Tiffany and her boy friend over for lunch. Nice guy I guess, but really not good enough for Tiff. Anyway she was telling about the investing philosophy of her investment club. If I remember correctly . . ."

"I heard that!" Tiffany had good ears and was just coming around the corner.

Winking at Rob, "He's never liked any of my boy friends. Cut me some slack Jakey. A girl's got to have a little fun."

"Jake was telling me about the philosophy of your investment club. Could you explain it," Rob asked.

"Sure. We are members of NAIC, National Association of Investors Corporation. They provide a lot of support, monthly magazine and such. There are four basic principles. Make regular investments, reinvest all earnings and dividends, invest in growth equities, and diversify. But like I said earlier the concept of options has never come up. Why do you think that is?"

"My guess," Rob responded, "is they are not familiar with how conservative and risk free a covered call transaction is. Like most people when they think of options trading they are thinking of buying rather than selling. But actually my strategy would be perfect for an investment club. I've worked out a rational process of stock selection and ranking. And having done it both ways, I much prefer the money tree concept. By the way Jake was just explaining his understanding of the concept. Can you join us?"

"No, I've got to get back to the front. But how about giving a presentation to our investment club?"

"Be glad to. Set it up and let me know." And she was off. "Okay Jake, tell me about the money tree concept. That's my first of two questions for you."

"Obviously it's entirely different from the traditional investing that you hear from John Bogle or learn in investment clubs. The key there is stock appreciation over time. With the money tree concept you are more interested in how much fruit you can pick off the tree rather than how tall the tree may grow. In the case of calls you are happy if your stock gets bought. And in the case of puts you may never even own the stock. I see definite advantages. You have short term relationships with stocks so you are not likely to get emotionally involved. And you get paid up front when you sell a call or put. That money is yours no matter what. Oh and one other thing. You make money even in a stagnant market. And perhaps even in a down market like that investment you showed me in Cott. You don't need stock appreciation to make money. That's about it. How did I do?"

"Very good. I think you've got it. Now here's your second question. What does the money tree concept have in common with investment clubs?"

Jake was surprised at the question. He finally understood how different the two concepts were. How could they have any thing in common?

"Gee professor, I'm drawing a blank. They seem to be entirely opposite." Glancing over his notes he suddenly saw the answer.

"Oh, I've got it. It's what you said we would cover next after the money tree concept. Building a qualified prospect list and ranking the stocks. I understand that's also the main topic of discussion in investment club meetings, the merits of various stock candidates for investing. Am I right?"

"Absolutely. The most important decision before selling a call or put is stock selection." Rob glanced at his watch. "I'm meeting Jean in 30 minutes. Let's talk about building a qualified prospect list and then we will cover ranking the stocks later.

"Remember, at this point we are simply building a qualified prospect list and organizing it into marketplace or technology areas with three or four companies in each area. We are like the owner of a major league baseball team. We want a lot of players on the farm team. And of course we want to develop player-prospects for each position. But just because a stock makes it onto the prospect list does not mean we are about to buy it. Many farm league players never make it to the big league. Using my software program we easily sort the list to determine our best prospects. I also continue to include on the prospect list stocks I have bought or on which I've sold a naked put. I continue to include them in the ranking process to be sure they are still viable.

"There is no limit to how many stocks you can have on your prospect list. But each stock you include must pass the following five tests:

- An options market exists for the stock

- Annual sales of at least $250 million

- Five year revenue growth of at least 15% per year

- Positive earnings at least 3 of the last 4 quarters

- Average daily trading volume of at least 200,000 shares per day.

"You have to search for good companies since they are not obvious. You should first look in an industry or market that you are familiar with. No matter what your background is, you probably can name thirty to fifty companies very quickly that touched your life in the last twenty-four hours one way or another. From the cereal you had for breakfast, the type of vehicle you drive, the brand of gas you use, the last store you shopped, to the computer on your desk, there are various companies that could have filled your needs. You picked certain ones because of a fuzzy feeling for the product or good advertising on the company's part. I like the computer and communications networking business. I therefore have a prospect list that is weighted heavily in the computer systems, software, networking, and semiconductor markets. I have supplemented this list with companies in the retail, defense, medical technology, and air transportation areas.

"Identify several marketplace or technology areas that you like and understand. There are a number of places to find these candidates. I always consider stocks that are in the highest volume of shares traded for the day as prospects. High volume is important for two reasons. First you want to always have a market for your stocks. High volume indicates high liquidity. Second, high volume indicates that the market has scrutinized the company very closely. When the market focuses intently on a company, all information available is reflected in the price of the stock. You can then conclude that the stock is accurately priced by the market. No hidden surprises are likely. Look also at the percent gainers and losers list for the day. Check the news. Why did a particular stock go up or down so much in one day? Maybe an analyst upgraded or downgraded the stock, the company beat or missed their earnings estimate, there is new competition, there is a take over rumor or the rumor has been dispelled, etc. There are many reasons. Something major happened and in many cases it is temporary so this may be an opportunity worth tracking.

"I also have found many prospects by looking at the major markets daily and weekly new low lists. Every company has a 52-week high and low. Stocks do go up and down. When good companies hit a new low this is the time to place them on your prospect list and start tracking them. At some point they will move up from this new low and that may be the time we want to get in. We want to buy low and sell calls as the stock moves up. All of this information is available in the Wall Street Journal."

Rob pulled a sheet of paper out of his notebook and handed it to Jake. "Here's a list of thirty stocks on my prospect list which I have arranged in ten groups of three. This is just an example. Actually I have over 100 stocks that I track as prospects. You will need to form your own list based on your particular interests and field of expertise."

Jake had written down the five tests for stocks to pass before being included on his prospect list. "Professor concerning the tests, how do I get that information?"

"No problem. The information is readily available on numerous web sites. For example www.wallstreetcity.com or www.cbsmarketwatch.com."

Rob's PDA rang just as Tiffany rounded the corner with an excited expression. "Yes Jean, I'm leaving in two minutes. Love you.

"Professor," Tiffany exclaimed. "I just talked to the president of our investment club. We had a cancellation and our planned guest speaker can not come tonight. Could you fill in?"

ROB GRAHAM PROSPECT LIST	
WalMart (WMT)	Oracle (ORCL)
Costco (COST)	Microsoft(MSFT)
Target (TGT)	Siebel Systems (SEBL)
Medimmune (MEDI)	McDATA Corp 'A' (MCDTA)
Lincare Holdings (LNCR)	Seagate Technology (STX)
Enzon Pharmaceuticals (ENZN)	Western Digital (WDC)
JDA Software Group (JDAS)	Cisco Systems (CSCO)
Network Associates (NET)	Extreme Networks (EXTR)
Citrix systems (CTXS)	Foundry Networks (FDRY)
Lockheed Martin (LMT)	Sun Micro (SUNW)
General Dynamics (GD)	Hewlett Packard (HWP)
Honeywell (HON)	Dell Computers (DELL)
Northwest Airlines (NWAC)	Cardinal Health (CAH)
Southwest Airlines (LUV)	Boston Scientific (BSX)
AirTran (AAI)	Medtronic (MDT)

7

Buy Low—Sell High

"Create your own vision of happiness."
Jean Groenke

The investment club met at the home of its president, Nicholas Gardner, a past president of Rotary and active citizen of Marco Island.

Tiffany introduced Rob and Jake to Nicholas and wife, Kris, as the members mingled and enjoyed Kris's punch and cookies. The beautiful home was at the end of a street, typical of Marco Island, with a wide canal on each side and bay to the front. The house was surrounded on three sides with water and was designed to take full advantage of the views.

Jake and Tiffany took seats as Nicholas called the meeting to order. "Tonight," he began, "we are pleased to have a retired finance professor and recent resident of Marco Island as our speaker. Please give your attention to Dr. Rob Graham."

There was friendly applause as Rob stood beside the flip chart facing the group of investors.

"Thank you Nicholas and members and especially Tiffany for inviting me tonight. It's always a pleasure to share investment information with interested, intelligent investors. I'm somewhat familiar with NAIC. I admire your dedication to periodic investing and your diligent analysis of individual stocks. As you know there are many very complicated and sophisticated methods of stock analysis. Over the course of my teaching career I've explored the intricacies of fundamental analysis and technical analysis. Each has its pros and cons. But in the final analysis what it all comes down to is that old cliché: *Buy Low—Sell High.*"

Rob continued. "When you look at the history of each stock in your portfolio you see that each was purchased at some point in a cycle which has now become evident. We can look back and see that some were bought at a low point in the cycle and then moved up. Some were bought at a high point in the cycle and then moved down. Those in the later group may have now moved back up. Over time your gain is greatest in those stocks which you bought at the low point of their cycles.

"Now the question I asked myself is 'Is there anyway to increase the odds that I am buying at the low point of the cycle?' Take the two extremes. At the end of each trading day there are stocks which have closed at a 52 week high. And there are also stocks that closed at a 52 week low. Assuming you have eliminated consideration of stocks with low liquidity, negative earnings or declining sales, which stocks are most likely to be at the bottom of their cycle?

"I offer no guaranties but I have personally been very successful with stocks moving up from their 52 week low.

"The formulas I will give you are to compute what I call Buy Limit and Buy Rank. These two values allow me very quickly to filter my prospect list and rank the stocks. For every stock you can get its lowest price of the past 52 weeks and its highest price. Let L stand for the 52 week low and H stand for the 52 week high. The Buy Limit formula is as follows." Rob wrote the following formula on the flip chart.

$$\text{Buy Limit} = L + .25\,(H - L)$$

"Ideally we would like to buy at L, the 52 week low. But we have to accept the fact that we cannot time the market and know that today's L will not be superseded by an even lower L tomorrow. But it is possible we can catch the stock on the way up from L. That's our objective here. The critical increment is .25(H - L). For example if a stock has a 52 week low of \$10 and a 52 week high of $40 then the critical increment is $7.50. That's computed by taking 25% of $40 minus $10. You might think of 7.50 as our window of opportunity. I would be interested in buying the stock in the price range from $10 to $17.50. As we get closer to $17.50, the *Buy Limit*, I begin losing interest in the stock. "At $17.50 it is too high. It's easy to see the trend when you are looking at a chart of the stock's prices. I'll show you one in just a moment.

"Now we use the Buy Limit in the following formula to compute the Buy Rank for each stock. Let's let BL stand for Buy Limit and CP stand for the Current Price of the stock. Notice that the denominator is the critical increment we computed to use in the last formula.

$$\text{Buy Rank} = \frac{10\,(\text{BL} - \text{CP})}{.25\,(\text{H} - \text{L})}$$

"When the current stock price is the same as the 52 week low the buy rank is 10. This is its maximum value. When the current stock price is the same as the 52 week high, the buy rank is negative 30. Our Buy Rank formula gives us a range of values on a scale from negative 30 to positive 10."

Rob drew the following on the flip chart below the two formulas.

| −30 | 0 | + 5 | +10 |

"A stock captures my attention with a Buy Rank between 10 and 5, moving down. A decreasing value in the Buy Rank indicates the stock is moving up in price and perhaps has started its next major up trend.

"For example using our example of a stock with 52 week low of $10 and 52 week high of $40, we computed the Buy Limit to be $17.50. Suppose the current price were $12. At that price we are well below our Buy Limit of $17.50. What is the Buy Rank? It is

10(17.50 - 12) which is 55 divided by 7.50. That's a Buy Rank of 7.33. As the current price rises closer to the Buy Limit the Buy Rank declines, approaching zero. For example a current price of $16 gives a Buy Rank of 2. A current price of $17 gives a Buy Rank of 0.66. And of course a current price of $17.50, the same as the Buy Limit, would give a Buy Rank of zero. So we are only interested in stocks with a positive Buy Rank. With my software program I easily compute the Buy Limit and Buy Rank of each stock on my prospect list. Then by clicking on the Buy Rank column my prospect list is sorted from best to worse.

"Are there any questions?"

Nicholas stood up, rubbing his chin and still looking at the simple formulas. "Rob," he said "this reminds me of Tiger Woods playing golf. He makes it look easy. With mastery comes ease of application and explanation. Does anyone have any comments or questions for Rob?"

"Did you originate these formulas," someone asked.

"Yes. I haven't seen them anywhere else," Rob replied. "When I started building my prospect list I began intuitively looking at the list each day of stocks trading at their 52 week low. Frequently the stock would be down because of a bit of sensational news and the market had over reacted. If the fundamentals were good I would add that stock to my prospect list. Also it seemed obvious to me that the greatest potential losses would come from stocks trading at 52 week highs such as the recent internet stocks."

A murmur went through the group as various members mentioned stocks that had resulted in losses.

"Oops," said Rob. "Did I hit a nerve?"

With a rueful smile Nicholas commented, "Our group got excited about Siebel several years ago. We had lots of discussions and analysis. Saw the president, Tom Siebel, interviewed on CNBC several times. Finally in February of 2001 we bought in at about $60 a share. It's been a downhill slide since."

"That's interesting," Rob replied. "Siebel is a stock that I've had considerable success with. I followed my Buy Limit and Buy Rank rules and did not get burned. I like the company. It is a provider of eBusiness applications, enabling organizations to sell to, market to, and service their customers across multiple channels. Would you like to take a look at my investment strategy with Siebel?"

All were interested in any way they could avoid their recent debacle with Siebel. Rob had noticed a large screen high definition TV behind the flip chart. "Nicholas, do you mind if I use your TV screen? I can show you my investment in Siebel."

Nicholas quickly turned the TV on and removed the flip chart. Rob punched commands into his PDA.

"Siebel caught my attention when it was on the NASDAQ new low list on 9-29-01. To do my analysis I needed some pertinent information about the stock. There are many places on the internet that provide this information for free. One favorite is www.cbs.marketwatch.com. Enter a stock symbol and then go to "Profile". Here's the key information I found back in September 2001."

The following information was displayed on the TV screen.

- SEBL stock price 17.22

- 52-week high - 119.87

- 52-week low - 12.24

- Revenue of over 1.7 Billion per year.

- Sales growth of 120% for the year.

- Earnings were positive the past five quarters.

- Average number of shares traded per day of over fifteen million shares.

Rob continued, "The fundamentals looked good. I placed it on my prospect list and checked its Buy Limit and Buy Rank. Here's the computation with my Buy Limit and Buy Rank Wizard."

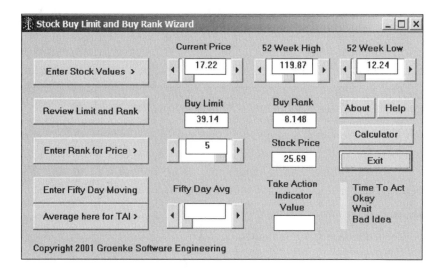

"The Buy Rank is 8.14, a nice positive number between 5 and 10. The Wizard also tells me what stock price relates to different Buy Ranks. For example here I entered a Buy Rank of 5 and see that the corresponding stock price would be 25.69.

"Everything looks good at this point. Before finally making the investment I also check to see where the stock is trading in relation to is fifty-day moving average. I like to get the very best odds I can," Rob explained. "I've found that it's not enough to have a stock with a good Buy Rank and good return for selling calls. Those are both critically important. But I want to be as sure as possible that the stock has actually started another up trend. So before investing I look at a picture of the stock. Here is where a picture could be worth thousands of dollars. I want to see the current price pass through the fifty day moving average. As long as the current price is leading the average down, don't invest. But when the price breaks above the fifty day moving average, I feel encouraged that we have begun an up trend. Does that make sense?

"Here is a chart for Siebel Systems for August 2001 through January 2004. Nice history. See how the stock has gone up and down.

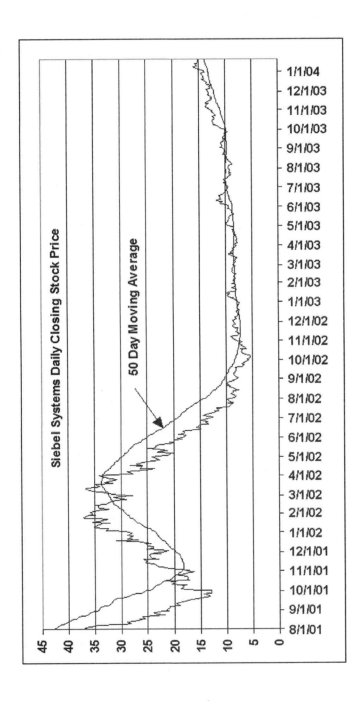

There are many periods of opportunity for both covered calls and naked puts with this example.

"Notice that in September 2001 it was trading below the fifty day moving average and moving up.

"Finally on October 17, 2001 with a price of 16.55 the stock crossed the fifty day moving average. Here's what happened." Rob punched on his PDA.

SIEBEL SYSTEMS	SEBL	FEB	MAY	AUG	NOV
10-17-01 B	1000	16.55	16555.00		-16555.00
10-17-01 S	10 Nov 17.50	2.10	2074.91		-14480.09

"I bought 1000 shares at $16.55 and sold covered calls one month out with a $17.50 strike price. The $2,074.91 I received is a 12.53% return for one month on the $16,555.00 investment. The return is a little higher if the stock is called." Rob paused to let this information sink in with the investment club.

As the group stared at the TV Tiffany was the first to ask a question. "Professor, would you explain covered calls? I'm not sure I understand exactly what happened."

"A key reason I bought Siebel, in addition to its good fundamentals and positive Buy Rank, was that it had good call option premiums. Before buying the 1000 shares I looked at several different options possibilities. I like to sell options with a strike price slightly above the purchase price which in this case is $17.50. I looked at the premiums for expiration dates in November, January, February and May. The returns are different for "If Sold" and "If Expired". If the option expires I only earn the option premium. But if the stock is called or sold I earn the premium plus a small amount of capital gain.

Here they are when the price of the stock was at $17.22:"

SIEBEL SYSTEMS SEBL FEB MAY AUG NOV			
Month/Strike	Bid	% If Sold	% If Expired
Nov 17.50	2.20	14.4	12.7
Jan 17.50	3.20	20.2	18.5
Feb 17.50	3.70	23.1	21.4
May 17.50	4.60	28.3	26.7

"On the day I did the analysis the market was offering to pay me $2.20 a share for the option to buy my shares at a price of $17.50 up to the third Friday in November, about one month later. I could have received $4.60 a share for a May 2002 expiration. The longer the expiration period the more money I could make. I opted to take a quick one month profit.

"You see," Rob continued, "my investment strategy involves a concept I call the money tree. Rather than being strictly interested in stock appreciation I pick money off the money tree on a continuous basis by selling options."

Looking at Nicholas, Rob asked, "Has the investment club ever considered selling options?"

"No," Nicholas replied, "and I'm not sure why. I have a general impression that options are very risky. But I don't see anything scary about what you just showed us with Siebel."

"Right," Rob agreed. "The value of the money tree approach can be seen by contrasting my investment in Siebel with the standard 'buy and hold' strategy. Here's the full picture."

SIEBEL SYSTEMS SEBL		FEB	MAY	AUG	NOV
10-17-01 B	1000	16.55	16555.00	-16555.00	
10-17-01 S	10 Nov 17.50	2.10	2074.91	-14480.09 CA	
10-17-01	10 JAN 17.50	1.70	1674.94	-12805.15 PE	
11-02-01 S	10 DEC 15.00	1.25	1224.95	-11580.20 PE	
11-07-01 B	1000	22.76	22760.00	-34340.20	
11-07-01 S	10 Nov 22.50	1.25	1224.95	-33115.25 CA	
11-16-01 C	1000	17.50	17480.41	-15634.84	
11-16-01 C	1000	22.50	22480.25	6845.41	
11-23-01 B	1000	24.04	24045.00	-17199.59	

The chart above flashed on the TV screen, covering the period from October 17, 2001 through November 23, 2001. After a little more work with his PDA Rob had the chart on the following page on the screen.

11-23-01 S	10 DEC 25.00	1.50	1474.95	-15724.64 CA
11-26-01 B	2000	24.93	49865.00	-65589.64
11-26-01 S	10 JAN 25.00	2.90	2874.90	-62714.74 CA
11-26-01 S	10 FEB 25.00	3.70	3674.86	-59039.88 CA
12-21-01 C	1000	25.00	24980.16	-34059.72
01-18-02 C	1000	25.00	24980.62	-9079.10
02-15-02 C	1000	25.00	24980.62	15901.52
07-17-02 S	10 AUG 10.00	.70	674.95	16576.47 PA
08-16-02 B	1000	10.00	10019.00	6557.47
08-21-02 S	10 SEP 10.00	.50	474.95	7032.42 CE
09-23-02 S	10 NOV 10.00	.15	124.98	7157.40 CE
11-13-02 S	10 DEC 10.00	.25	224.97	7382.37 CE
12-13-02 S	10 JAN 10.00	.30	274.97	7657.34 CE
12-16-02 S	10 JAN 7.50	.65	624.98	8282.32 PE
01-17-03 S	10 FEB 10.00	.25	224.97	8507.29 CE
02-21-03 S	10 MAR 10.00	.20	174.98	8682.27 CE
03-21-03 S	10 MAY 10.00	.55	524.95	9207.22 CE
04-07-03 S	10 AUG 7.50	.90	874.95	10082.17 PE
05-12-03 S	10 NOV 7.50	.55	524.96	10607.13 PE
05-19-03 S	10 AUG 10.00	.50	474.95	11082.08 CE
08-18-03 S	10 NOV 10.00	.70	679.98	11762.06 CA
11-21-03 C	1000	10.00	9980.53	$21,742.59

Rob explained his notations. "My first goal with any investment is to have a positive cash flow. My second goal is to have a *very* positive cash flow. When I make an investment I am buying something so that is cash out. I show that as a negative balance in the last column. As I make money with the investment by selling options or having stock called, that's cash inflow which eventually gives me a positive balance in the last column. An S in the first column indicates the sale of an option. At the end of that row you can see the type and disposition of the option sale. For example the sale on October 17, 2001 was a call option which was assigned (CA). 'Assigned' means my 1000 shares were purchased by the option holder, in this case for $17.50 per share. That result is shown on 11-16-2001, the third Friday that month, where I have a cash inflow of $17,480.41.

"Over this two year period my maximum investment was $65,589.64 on November 26, 2001 but by the following February I had a positive balance. For most of the two years I had nothing at risk and made a profit of $21,742.59.

"By imposing the Buy Limit and Buy Rank restraint on myself I avoided buying Siebel at any time other than the low point in its cycle. Siebel has had a negative Buy Rank since about October of 2002. So I shifted to other stocks in my prospect list which have a positive Buy Rank. But as time moves forward you will notice that the 52 week low will be moving up. This will cause the Buy Rank to become more positive and before too long it again is a prime candidate. In the mean time it is a good candidate for naked puts at a strike price that is at or below the Buy Limit. This is a good way to get back in for the next cycle and pluck some money from the tree while you wait."

One of the club members had pulled his chair up closer to the TV and was intently analyzing the Siebel investment. "Professor, I've got a question."

"Yes sir. Fire away," Rob responded.

"Because you sold those call options in October 2001, you were forced to sell 2000 shares of Siebel, half at $17.50 and half at $22.50. Consequently you missed the big run up to over $35 just a few months later."

"Yes, that's true," Rob agreed. "But only if you would have sold at that high. How often is that done?

"Which would you say is more rewarding? Is it better to have the thrill of the ride up and down or is it better to steadily pick money off the money tree by selling options? That's a decision for each investor to make."

There was a chatter from the club members as they began discussing the merits of selling options. For most it was a brand new concept. Nicholas stood up to regain control of the meeting. "Rob, you have certainly given us a challenging presentation. This is a strategy we need to discuss. But just one final question so I'm sure I understand. You apparently make money in the stock market by selling options. Are you not interested in market appreciation?"

Rob thought for a few seconds searching for the right words to explain his strategy. "I am interested in market appreciation but not for the same reason as most investors. Your club for example spent a lot of time analyzing investment options and then settled on Siebel at $60. You tried to pick a stock that was going up over the long run. And eventually you may be right. Although you might note that investors who bought RCA at its high point in the 1920s are still in a loss position.

"Basically I think you set yourself a very difficult task when you try to pick market winners. The very best stock analysts are seldom right more than 50% of the time. Look at how few mutual funds out perform index funds. And none out perform index funds on a consistent basis.

"But having said that, I am careful about stock selection. I require a positive Buy Rank based on the formulas I showed you. That is a very stringent requirement that has served me well, although certainly not perfect. I've been burned several times with what I thought were good companies. However any loss that I incurred because the stock went down was cushioned by the premiums I garnered by selling calls.

"There are basically two reasons I am very careful with stock selection. And these are not the typical reasons you would hear from the average investor or market analyst. Most investors, like this investment club, are trying to buy the right stocks for price appreciation. Frankly, as I said, I think that's just too difficult for anyone to do on a consistent long term basis. The two reasons I want stocks likely to go up are: 1) Avoid losses and 2) The option premiums are higher if the market has positive expectations for the stock. My return on selling options is so good that I don't really need stock appreciation. What I'm doing is playing good defense as I consistently pick money off the money tree. As demonstrated by the last example, I sold calls on my SEBL position for over a year while waiting for the stock to go up. There was little appreciation during this time but I averaged 2.25% return per month."

Nicholas walked over to Rob and held out his hand. "Thank you so much for your presentation. I'm sure our club will benefit. Our track record is actually pretty good despite having bought a few stocks at the wrong time. I can definitely see the value of your formulas."

"I've enjoyed the evening. Perhaps I should leave you with one cautionary note."

8

A Note of Caution

"You should invest in companies that even a fool can run,
because someday a fool will."
Warren Buffett

"I want to emphasize," Rob continued, "that no stock market system is full proof. You have all been impressed with the return available by selling options.

"But there is always the clear and present danger that the stocks you have selected can go down and totally wipe out any profit you've made from selling options.

"A prime example of what can happen in the real world is the trade experience I had with ValuJet (VJET). You already guessed it. I owned the stock when one of their planes crashed. Lets review what happened.

"On 05-03-96 I purchased 2000 shares of VJET for $13.50 each and sold December 12.50 calls for a premium of $3.375. A gain of 25% if expired and 19% if called out in seven months. On May 11, 1996 a ValuJet DC9 crashed into the Everglades in Florida with no survivors. The price of the stock was affected when all of Valu-Jets planes were grounded. Since I had losses built into my plan I took action on 06-18-96 and closed out my call options (bought them back) and sold the stock the next day. This is noted in line two of the table as CC for Closed Call.

"What started out to be a good trade turned into a sizable loss with zero warning. Tragic and unforeseen events will happen when least expected. Have some built into your plan.

"I do everything I can to protect against stock market surprises. In fact I have losses built into my plan. I'll tell more about that later.

"I keep this account summary with me as constant reminder of what can happen"

The following chart flashed on the TV screen.

	VALUJET VJET	MAR	JUN	SEP DEC
05-03-96 B	2000	13.50	27029.00	-27029.00
05-03-96 S	20 DEC 12.500	3.375	6664.77	-20364.23 CC
06-18-96 B	20 DEC 12.500	.75	1550.00	-21914.23
06-19-96 S	2000	6.625	13221.00	-8693.23

9

Jake's Prospect List

"Invest in companies, not stocks."
Peter Lynch

The next morning Jake hurried out to purchase a copy of the Wall Street Journal. As they left the investment club meeting the night before Rob had suggested he build a qualified prospect list of at least 15 companies, which met the criteria for sales, earnings and liquidity. For each company he was to compute the Buy Limit and Buy Rank.

After last night's session with the investment club, Jake was more motivated that ever to learn everything he could about the professor's options strategy. He knew the professor had a lot more to teach him, but he also knew the importance of getting the basics down. So he very dutifully went about his homework assignment, building a qualified prospect list. Flipping through the Wall Street Journal he began listing companies that he recognized. Soon he had over 50 companies. Next he grouped the companies into market place or technology areas. In some cases he was not sure what category to place the company. He went to google.com and checked the company's web site to be sure. While on the internet he did a search for pharmaceutical companies and discovered a list of 213 companies. To keep his analysis manageable he decided to limit his list to five categories and find three qualified candidates in each category. His categories were retail stores, software systems, pharmaceuticals, book stores, and airlines.

Going through his notes he found the five tests that each company must pass before it could be on his prospect list. He decided to make a spreadsheet listing his potential prospects down the left side of the page the five tests across the top. These were:

- An options market exists for the stock

- Annual sales of at least $250 million

- Five year revenue growth of at least 15% per year

- Positive earnings at least 3 of the last 4 quarters

- Average daily trading volume of at least 200,000 shares per day.

The professor had recommended several internet sites for company information. Looking through his notes Jake found two:

www.wallstreetcity.com and

www.cbs.marketplace.com

After eliminating the companies that did not pass the five point test he selected what appeared to him to be the top three in each category. Going back to the web he quickly gathered the 52-Week High, 52-Week Low and Last Price for each stock. His next step would be to compute Buy Limit and Buy Rank using the formulas the professor had given him. With a sinking feeling he looked at the two formulas he would need to use.

$$\text{Buy Limit} = L + .25\,(H - L)$$

$$\text{Buy Rank} = \frac{10\,(BL - CP)}{.25\,(H - L)}$$

Jake's Prospect List						
Company	Stock Symbol	52WK High	52WK Low	Last Price	Buy Limit	Buy Rank
Walmart	WMT	61.31	50.50	57.97		
Costco wholesale	COST	40.42	28.83	37.04		
Target	TGT	45.86	28.50	45.29		
Oracle	ORCL	15.51	10.65	11.70		
Microsoft	MSFT	30.00	23.59	25.18		
Siebel Systems	SEBL	16.19	7.48	10.91		
Medtronic	MDT	52.92	42.90	49.36		
Boston Scientific	BSX	45.31	20.27	39.85		
ImClone	IMCL	48.93	14.48	45.27		
Barns & Noble	BKS	36.26	17.38	33.34		
Borders	BGP	24.70	13.75	24.03		
Amazon	AMZN	61.15	24.13	42.13		
Southwest Airlines	LUV	19.69	12.88	13.44		
Northwest Airlines	NWAC	15.21	6.30	8.87		
AirTran Hldgs	AAI	20.84	5.85	11.08		

As he was about to start the long process of running the formulas on each company, the phone rang.

With his mind still on the daunting computing task before him he slowly picked up the phone. "Hello."

"Jake, this is Rob Graham."

"Professor, good morning. I'm just working on my prospect list."

"I thought you might be. Have you started computing Buy Limit and Buy Rank?"

"I was about to but I began getting a headache just thinking about all the computations."

"Not a problem," Rob assured him. "Just go to my web site and download my software. You will be able to easily compute Buy Limit and Buy Rank."

Rob gave him the web site—KellerPublishing.com—and Jake's headache immediately began to ease. A few minutes later the table was complete with Buy Limit and Buy Rank scores.

As Jake became familiar with the software program he discovered that he could easily sort the whole list by any column.

"Katie, could you come take a look at this." They were usually within hollering distance of each other.

As Katie looked over his shoulder at the computer screen Jake explained his prospect list.

"These are fifteen stocks that we might buy. I'm analyzing each stock based on its current price compared to its 52 week high and 52 week low." Jake showed Katie the list with the last two columns blank. "Now watch what happens when I use the professor's software program" The prospect list appeared with Buy Limit and Buy Rank computed.

Jake's Prospect List With Buy Limit and Buy Rank Values						
Company	Stock Symbol	52WK High	52WK Low	Last Price	Buy Limit	Buy Rank
Walmart	WMT	61.31	50.50	57.97	53.20	-17.64
Costco wholesale	COST	40.42	28.83	37.04	31.73	-18.33
Target	TGT	45.86	28.50	45.29	32.84	-28.69
Oracle	ORCL	15.51	10.65	11.70	11.87	1.36
Microsoft	MSFT	30.00	23.59	25.18	25.19	.08
Siebel Systems	SEBL	16.19	7.48	10.91	9.66	-5.75
Medtronic	MDT	52.92	42.90	49.36	45.41	-15.79
Boston Scientific	BSX	45.31	20.27	39.85	26.53	-21.28
ImClone	IMCL	48.93	14.48	45.27	23.09	-25.75
Barns & Noble	BKS	36.26	17.38	33.34	22.10	-23.81
Borders	BGP	24.70	13.75	24.03	16.49	-27.55
Amazon	AMZN	61.15	24.13	42.13	33.39	-9.45
Southwest Airlines	LUV	19.69	12.88	13.44	14.58	6.71
Northwest Airlines	NWAC	15.21	6.30	8.87	8.53	-1.54
AirTran Hldgs	AAI	20.84	5.85	11.08	9.80	-3.96

"Now here's another trick I can do with the professor's software." Jake clicked on the Buy Rank column. The list was automatically rearranged so that the Buy Rank column was sorted from most positive to most negative value.

Jake's Prospect List Sorted by Buy Rank						
Company	Stock Symbol	52WK High	52WK Low	Last Price	Buy Limit	Buy Rank
Southwest Airlines	LUV	19.69	12.88	13.44	14.58	6.71
Oracle	ORCL	15.51	10.65	11.70	11.87	1.36
Microsoft	MSFT	30.00	23.59	25.18	25.19	.08
Northwest Airlines	NWAC	15.21	6.30	8.87	8.53	-1.54
AirTran Hldgs	AAI	20.84	5.85	11.08	9.80	-3.96
Siebel Systems	SEBL	16.19	7.48	10.91	9.66	-5.75
Amazon	AMZN	61.15	24.13	42.13	33.39	-9.45
Medtronic	MDT	52.92	42.90	49.36	45.41	-15.79
Walmart	WMT	61.31	50.50	57.97	53.20	-17.64
Costco wholesale	COST	40.42	28.83	37.04	31.73	-18.33
Boston Scientific	BSX	45.31	20.27	39.85	26.53	-21.28
Barns & Noble	BKS	36.26	17.38	33.34	22.10	-23.81
ImClone	IMCL	48.93	14.48	45.27	23.09	-25.75
Borders	BGP	24.70	13.75	24.03	16.49	-27.55
Target	TGT	45.86	28.50	45.29	32.84	-28.69

Jake started explaining Buy Limit and Buy Rank. "The Buy Limit is the maximum price we would pay for a stock. When you see that the Last Price exceeds the Buy Limit then the stock is already too high. Our objective is to buy low and the buy limit keeps us on the low end."

Katie recognized one of the stocks. "I see you have ImClone on the list. Just how bad is a Buy Rank of -25.75?"

"Not acceptable. Notice that the Buy Limit is 23.09. That's the most we would pay for ImClone at this time."

"Oh," Katie said with a slight frown. "That's too bad. You know we have 500 shares of ImClone I inherited from Aunt Candace. Wonder how much we could make selling calls on those 500 shares?"

"That's right," Jake replied. "I had forgotten about that stock. And I'll bet Martha Stewart wishes she had never heard of it." He shook his head sadly remembering the sensational court case. "Even though we wouldn't buy it at the current price we can consider selling calls. I'll do the computations while you fix us a cup of coffee."

Jake found the formulas he had used on his first homework assignment.

$$\text{If Sold} = \frac{(\text{Strike Price} + \text{Premium} - \text{Purchase Price})}{\text{Purchase Price}}$$

$$\text{If Expired} = \frac{\text{Premium}}{\text{Purchase Price}}$$

A few minutes later Katie was back with coffee and cinnamon rolls as Jake put the final touches on his analysis.

"ImClone closed today at $45.27. I decided to use that as our purchase price in the formula although since we inherited the stock we don't really have any investment cost in it. For tax purposes if we were to sell we would have the cost basis used in the estate tax return but I don't know what that is right now."

ImClone Systems IMCL			Date: 3-16-04
Month/Strike	Bid	% If Sold	**% If Expired**
Apr 45	2.65	5.2	5.8
Apr 50	1.00	12.6	2.2
May 45	3.80	7.7	8.3
May 50	2.00	14.8	4.4
Aug 45	5.50	11.2	12.1
Aug 50	3.50	18.1	7.7

"Hold on now. Let me be sure I understand this." Katie tapped the Aug 45 row. "What's a 5.50 bid mean?" Before Jake could answer she said "Jake, what's 500 times $5.50?" Jake smiled as he did the computation. Sometimes his wife surprised him with her quick insights.

"The answer is $2,750. That's the amount we could receive by selling calls on our 500 shares of ImClone. Today is March 16, 2004. August options will expire on August 20, 2004, that's the 3rd Friday in August."

Katie followed the August 45 line across to 11.2 and 12.1 "Does this mean that return for selling the calls will be either 11.2% or 12.1%? Why is there a difference?"

The question hearkened back to Jake's first homework assignment. He wrote down the two formulas and began explaining the difference.

$$\text{If Sold} = \frac{(\text{Strike Price} + \text{Premium} - \text{Purchase Price})}{\text{Purchase Price}}$$

$$\text{If Expired} = \frac{\text{Premium}}{\text{Purchase Price}}$$

"Only one of two things will happen and in either case we get to keep the $2,750." Jake noticed that Katie was looking at the kitchen. She had recently mentioned some remodeling plans if only they had the extra money. "Uh, Katie, you were asking about the difference between 11.2% and 12.1%. Look I'll show you. See the two formulas. To compute the gain if the call expires, meaning the stock is not called by the option holder because the market price is $45 or less on August 20, simply divide the premium by the purchase price. That would be $5.50 divided by $45.27." Jake showed her the answer of 12.117.

"Let's compute the gain "If Sold" for the August 45 calls. That would happen if the stock price is above $45 on August 20. Using the other formula it would be $45.00 plus $5.50 minus $45.27 divided by $45.27." Using his calculator Jake showed Katie the answer of 11.26%.

"Okay," Katie said, "I see the difference. If the stock is called you have to take into account the difference between the strike price and the purchase price. Since the strike price is a little less than the purchase price we don't make quite as much if the stock is called."

"That's right," Jake replied. "You've got it." Jake took a bite of a cinnamon roll and puzzled over the table. "But what I don't understand is which option should we sell. The April 45 option would give us a return of over 5% for just a month. April expirations are just one month from today." He was concentrating so hard on the ImClone analysis he didn't hear Katie leave to answer the phone. She soon came bustling back with a big grin.

"Jake you are not going to believe who was on the phone.

"Rob and Jean Graham have just invited us over to their condo for lunch tomorrow. They have someone they want us to meet."

10

What's the Best Option— The Magic Chart

"Success is the progressive realization of a worthy goal."
Earl Nightingale

Riding up the glass elevator to the Graham's penthouse condo, Katie and Jake had a panoramic view of Marco Island. On their left was the Yacht Club at the foot of the Jolley Bridge, which connected the island to the mainland of southwest Florida. They saw a small jet which had taken off from the Naples Airport, about 20 miles to the north. The owner apparently wanted a view of Marco before making a sharp turn to the north. On their right they could see all the way to Goodland, a small community also on the island with another bridge connecting to the mainland. The elevator was for the exclusive use of the two penthouse condos at the top of the most recent luxury tower built on the beach. As they stepped out onto the open foyer they had views of the beautiful crescent beach to the north and the south.

"I wonder who they want us to meet," said Katie as Jake pushed the door bell. Before the melodic chime had ended Jean Graham opened the door and warmly welcomed them in.

"Come in," she smiled. "We are so glad you could come over. I've heard about you, Jake, from my husband. And Katie, what a beautiful sundress. Did you get it here on the island? Jake, Rob is on the balcony. Why don't you go on out. There's a glass of ice tea waiting for you out there. We'll join you in a moment." Jean had the graceful movements of a ballerina as she motioned Jake in the direction of the balcony.

Jake left the two women to get acquainted as he walked across the wide expanse of the Great Room. The view outside was magnificent but he was mainly intrigued by the wide collection of paintings and artifacts. He quickly noticed items from the Orient, Australia and Europe. *World travelers*, he decided.

As he stepped out onto the balcony he had the commanding view of the gulf to the west. The noon sun was just high enough to begin casting its rays on the west balcony. Rob called from the corner to the north. "Come around here Jake. We can have the shade and still enjoy the view."

As Jake took a comfortable seat, Rob set his book aside and said, "We've always been so rushed in our prior meetings. Maybe this afternoon we can have a good visit. I've wanted to ask you about your book. You mentioned that you sold your CPA firm and moved to Marco to write a novel."

Mention of the CPA firm brought back many mixed emotions for Jake. There was the satisfaction of serving his clients and the frustration of having to jump through so many senseless—and sometimes contradictory—hoops. *Like a trained show dog,* he thought.

"Yes, well, I seem to have writer's block here lately. The novel idea comes from my work experience. After graduation from the University of Minnesota, I worked for a small accounting firm while preparing to pass the test to be a Certified Public Accountant. The company I was working for had experienced accountants who specialized in auditing, small business "write-up" work and management advisory services. It just so happened that they were weak in the area of tax planning. That was the void that I filled. I was soon the tax specialist. When I started my own firm I continued on in the tax field.

"Just about every year there would be major changes in the tax law. At CPE classes, that's continuing professional education classes, these new tax laws were jokingly referred to as 'The Accountants and Tax Lawyers Relief Act'. That always rankled me. The thought that I was somehow receiving a government subsidy.

And then I had to agree that I was indeed receiving a subsidy. The whole tax industry, from the simplest tax preparer to the most elaborate scheme for corporate, estate or personal tax avoidance, is a clear example of what's become known as corporate welfare. So unnecessary when we could have a simplified system based on sales or property values."

Looking down at the gulf Jake could see a pelican diving for a fish. *Now that's an honest living,* he thought. *No bureaucracies and no taxes. The pelican keeps what it earns and earns what it keeps.*

"So my novel is based in the world of public accountants and hopefully exposes what I see as serious flaws in the tax system."

"That's interesting," Rob commented. "But it's liable to get you the nick name of 'Don Quixote'. So many different groups have such a vested interest in a complicated tax system that I doubt it could ever be changed." Rob stood up and looked out at the gulf and down the beach.

"Jake, bring the binoculars over. They are right there by your chair. Looks like a sail boat race is about to begin."

Jake joined Rob at the railing and they took turns looking at the sailboats in fierce competition about half way to the horizon. Looking down the beach they could see sun bathers of all descriptions and swimmers enjoying the surf. Just below them a volley ball game was in progress with six girls playing against six local guys. The girl's team was in training for the summer Olympics and would no doubt handily defeat the local champions.

"You know Jake," Rob said, handing him the binoculars, "when there is so much beauty in the world it's hard to get caught up in crusades to make changes. If there is a drawback to living on Marco maybe that's it. It's so easy to go with the flow and enjoy life. I enjoy focusing on my investments and spending time with Jean. We keep up with the kids and grandkids. What more does a man need in life? Maybe that's why you have writer's block on your novel. Lighten up. Enjoy life."

Jean and Katie joined them with a platter of sandwiches and pitcher of iced tea. "My specialty," said Jean. "Turkey on wheat with provolone cheese, lettuce, tomatoes and mayonnaise. I hope you like them."

Rob embraced Katie with a friendly hug. "So you are the reason my former student here received a B instead of an A in Finance 101. Well Jake, I can certainly understand your predicament." They all laughed, enjoying the conversation along with the food.

As they finished eating the sandwiches Katie was the first to broach the subject of options. "Rob, we've been learning about your investment strategy. Last night when you called, Jake was explaining to me his understanding of the strategy and we were stumped by a particular problem. Do you mind if we ask you a question?"

"Sure. I thought you might have some questions. I will be glad to share what I've learned about the options market. I don't offer any guarantees but it has sure worked for us."

Jake pulled the sheet of paper out of his pocket on which he had computed the various strike prices and dates for the 500 shares of ImClone he and Katie owned. He unfolded the paper and handed it to the professor.

ImClone Systems IMCL Date: 3-16-04			
Month/Strike	Bid	% If Sold	% If Expired
Apr 45	2.65	5.2	5.8
Apr 50	1.00	12.6	2.2
May 45	3.80	7.7	8.3
May 50	2.00	14.8	4.4
Aug 45	5.50	11.2	12.1
Aug 50	3.50	18.1	7.7

"Professor, we have 500 shares of ImClone which we inherited several years back. I did the computations using yesterday's closing price of $45.27 as the purchase price in the formulas. We are ready to sell calls on this stock. But how do we figure which of these six possibilities to select?"

Rob smiled. "ImClone, interesting company. I have used ImClone in many examples the past few years. Seems to go up and down a lot and is at the same price it was three years ago. That has not helped all of the folks that have bought and held. So which option should you select? You need my Magic Chart. Just a moment I'll get you a copy." Rob walked into his office and returned a moment later.

"What is a good premium for a covered call? That question plagued me for the first couple of years I was selling options. This area is mostly science and a little art. Our goal in selling calls is to generate a number of small gains on a continuous basis. If you want a larger premium the time factor will be longer. *Time IS Money*. How do we strike a balance between time and the overall gain? Through experience on simulating multiple option cycles and allowing for losses I have developed the following rate of return rate table for option premiums. This table is structured by current month and allows you to quickly determine if the rate of return on the option being considered is acceptable. It does not consider risk, so picking the right stock is also key. For improving our odds of picking the right stock we use the Buy Limit and Buy Rank computations. This table has successfully generated an average gain of 25% or more per year over a ten-year period."

Rob handed Jake an index size card with a chart on the front and the back. One side was for the months January through June. The other side had the months July through December.

Jake found the March column on side one. He went down the column to April and then across to the required percentages. One month out required a return of 6.8 if sold and 5.4 if expired. The corresponding returns he had computed for ImClone were

5.2 and 5.8, good enough if the options expired but not quite good enough if the options were called. Next he looked down the March column to May. For two months out the chart required a

THE MAGIC CHART – SIDE ONE								
MONTHS TO EXP.	IF SOLD	IF EXP.	JAN	FEB	MAR	APR	MAY	JUN
1	6.8	5.4	FEB	MAR	APR	MAY	JUN	JUL
2	8.4	6.7	MAR	APR	MAY	JUN	JUL	AUG
3	10.0	8.0	APR	MAY	JUN	JUL	AUG	SEP
4	11.6	09.3	MAY	JUN	JUL	AUG	SEP	OCT
5	13.4	10.7	JUN	JUL	AUG	SEP	OCT	NOV
6	15.0	12.0	JUL	AUG	SEP	OCT	NOV	DEC
7	16.6	13.3	AUG	SEP	OCT	NOV	DEC	JAN
8	18.4	14.7	SEP	OCT	NOV	DEC	JAN	FEB
9	20.0	16.0	OCT	NOV	DEC	JAN	FEB	MAR

THE MAGIC CHART – SIDE TWO								
MONTHS TO EXP.	IF SOLD	IF EXP.	JUL	AUG	SEP	OCT	NOV	DEC
1	6.8	5.4	AUG	SEP	OCT	NOV	DEC	JAN
2	8.4	6.7	SEP	OCT	NOV	DEC	JAN	FEB
3	10.0	8.0	OCT	NOV	DEC	JAN	FEB	MAR
4	11.6	09.3	NOV	DEC	JAN	FEB	MAR	APR
5	13.4	10.7	DEC	JAN	FEB	MAR	APR	MAY
6	15.0	12.0	JAN	FEB	MAR	APR	MAY	JUN
7	16.6	13.3	FEB	MAR	APR	MAY	JUN	JUL
8	18.4	14.7	MAR	APR	MAY	JUN	JUL	AUG
9	20.0	16.0	APR	MAY	JUN	JUL	AUG	SEP

return of 8.4 and 6.7. Again he was in good shape if the options expired but not quite good enough if the options were called. For August, five months out, he noted the chart required returns of 13.4 and 10.7.

"Professor, it looks like our best bet is with a $45 strike price because the $50 strike has such a low return for the If Expired case. But I'm still uncertain whether April, May or August is best for the $45 strike."

"Yes, my chart does not always give clear cut answers. It's a guide. Remember that time is money. In this case I would be tempted to take 5% for one month. Of course August is also tempting because it's nice to get over 10% for five months."

"What if our 500 shares of ImClone get called," asked Katie. "What if it goes up to $60 a share and someone else gets the benefit of all that appreciation?"

"That may well happen," Rob responded. "In fact you can certainly expect it to happen on at least some of your calls. But there is no way of knowing in advance which stocks will go up sharply. My strategy, as I mentioned earlier, is *to generate a number of small gains on a continuous basis.*

"Look again at Jake's computations for the percentage gain on the August 45 contract. Now ask yourself a basic question. Do you want to hold the stock without selling a call option on the chance that it may go up, knowing that it could just as easily go down as up? Or do you want to lock in a gain of at least 11.2% for a period of five months? That's better than you could get on a CD for several years.

"To specifically answer your question about what to do if your stock gets called, that's the purpose of having a prospect list. Your cash position is greater by, first, the $2,750 you receive from selling the calls and, second, by the sell of 500 shares for $45.00 a share. That's a total of $25,250. A stock that has risen sharply may now be above the Buy Limit and not have a satisfactory Buy Rank. If so you would use the money to buy a different stock with a good Buy Rank. Now you have the compounding effect of selling calls on stock purchased with the premium as well as the principle.

"Since it looks like you may be about to make your first foray into the options market, we had better talk about some of the technical terms you will encounter."

"Wait a minute," Jean interjected. "How about a slice of key lime pie for dessert. And I think it's getting a little warm here. Why don't we move inside and be more comfortable."

As they moved inside Katie commented to Jake, "Maybe we can plant our own money tree, starting with those 500 shares of Im-Clone?"

11

Selling Calls and Puts

"That some should be rich shows that others may become rich,
and hence is just encouragement to industry and enterprise."
Abe Lincoln

As the two couples settled down on luxurious leather couches, Rob proceeded to explain the technical aspects of options trading.

"Options are traded in the financial world the same as stocks at the Chicago Board Options Exchange (CBOE), American Stock Exchange (AMEX), Philadelphia and Pacific exchanges. Option orders are placed in your brokerage account and executed on an appropriate exchange. Not all stocks have options, so one needs to check availability by asking a stockbroker or accessing a quote service over the Internet such as at www.wallstreetcity.com or www.cboe.com.

"Buying and selling options is a little different from buying and selling stock. You usually just buy and sell stocks at a desired price. Option orders however require additional specifications such as expiration month, strike price, and intent (open or closing transaction). This information is communicated through the option symbol and specification of the order being placed.

"Stock and Index option symbols are composed of several different components representing the underlying security and information about the specific option contract. The first two or three letters of an option symbol are the option root, followed by the expiration month code, followed by the strike price code. Strike prices can vary depending on such factors as stock splits and sharp price moves etc. NYSE stocks use their stock symbol as their option root. For example Johnson & Johnson is JNJ, AT&T

is T, Boeing is BA, and Wal-Mart is WMT. NASDAQ stocks use three letter option roots assigned by the exchange. For example the option root for Applied Materials is ANQ and for Microsoft is MSQ.

"So an Option Symbol is composed of the Option Root, followed by month code, followed by strike price code."

Rob paused, noticing the confused looks from Jake and Katie. Jean broke the awkward silence with a suggestion. "Rob, dear, why don't you use the Illustrator I gave you for your birthday?"

"Good suggestion. Maybe this will help, Jake and Katie." With that he picked up what looked like leather bound book. Opening it he pushed a button and a large painting on the wall nearest them, a beautiful impressionist painting of a family skiing in the Swiss Alps, turned into a clear three foot by five foot screen. As Rob wrote in the Illustrator the information appeared on the screen for all to see.

"Here's the basic notation for expiration month codes," Rob said as he accessed a database. For each month there is one letter of the alphabet to signify a Call and a different letter to signify a Put.

	CALLS	PUTS
January	A	M
February	B	N
March	C	O
April	D	P
May	E	Q
June	F	R
July	G	S
August	H	T
September	I	U
October	J	V
November	K	W
December	L	X

"Then we use the letters again for stock price codes. One letter of the alphabet represents three possible prices. You will quickly get the hang of it."

A	5, 105, 205	N	70, 170, 270
B	10, 110, 210	O	75, 175, 275
C	15, 115, 215	P	80, 180, 280
D	20, 120, 220	Q	85, 185, 285
E	25, 125, 225	R	90, 190, 290
F	30, 130, 230	S	95, 195, 295
G	35, 135, 235	T	100, 200, 300
H	40, 140, 240	U	7.50, 37.50, 67.50
I	45, 145, 245	V	12.50, 42.50, 72.50
J	50, 150, 250	W	17.50, 47.50, 77.50
K	55, 155, 255	X	22.50, 52.50, 82.50
L	60, 160, 260	Y	27.50, 57.50, 87.50
M	65, 165, 265	Z	32.50, 62.50, 92.50

"Notice how this works in the following examples. In the first one, WMTLJ, the WMT stands for Wal-Mart, the "L" stands for December Call, and the J indicates a price of 50, 150 or 250, whichever one makes sense relative to the price of Wal-Mart stock. Of course that's 50.

WMTLJ Wal-Mart December 50 Call

WMTXI Wal-Mart December 45 Put

INQGZ Intel July 32.50 Call

INQOF Intel March 30 Put

MSQIN Microsoft September 70 Call

MSQXL Microsoft December 60 Put

THD AT&T August 20 Call

TVW AT&T October 17.50 Put

"Options quotes can be found in the newspaper or on the Internet. Two sites on the internet that I use often are www.cboe.com or www.wallstreetcity.com."

Rob paused. "I'll print out a copy of this for you. But don't worry about memorizing it. It will all be second nature after you've done a few trades. Do you want to keep going?"

12

Placing the Trade

When buying and selling are controlled by legislation, the
first things to be bought and sold are legislators.
P. J. O'Rourke

Jake nodded agreement and Rob continued. "Now before you run off to place your trade, it might be good to understand how option orders should be placed."

"When placing option trading orders it is very important to state exactly what is intended. If a mistake is made and you execute a wrong trade you may incur a loss to undo it.

"Option orders like stock orders can be placed in your brokerage account over the phone by calling a trader, over the phone with direct keypad input, or over the Internet with on line access to your account. No matter which way you trade the way an order is placed is important. I'll put on the screen some basic definitions."

As Rob pushed points in the notebook the following items appeared on the screen.

Sell to Open—You are opening a short position for a specific option. For example this is what you use to write a covered call.

Buy to Close—You are buying back an option you previously sold, to close out the option. For example this is what you would do if you did not want your stock to be called. Also, you would want to do this if you want to sell the stock. Selling the stock without buying back the call option would leave you in a high risk uncovered position.

Buy to Open—You are opening a long position for a specific option. For example this is what you do when you are taking a leveraged position by buying the option instead of the stock.

<u>Sell to Close</u>—You are closing a long position for a specific option. For example this is what you do to capture a gain on your leveraged position.

<u>Market order</u>—The order will be executed at the next available bid price. Use this to buy or sell immediately.

<u>Limit order</u>—The order is executed at the limit price or better if possible.

<u>For the day</u>—The order will expire at the end of the trading day.

<u>All or none (AON)</u>—Buy or sell the number of contracts specified. This condition is used to reduce the possibility of trading only one or a small number of contracts in a multiple contract order. Additional orders may increase your overall commission cost.

<u>Good till canceled (GTC)</u>—The order is open until it is canceled. Most brokerage firms will close GTC orders after ninety days.

"Considering what we've learned so far, your order to sell calls on your 500 shares of Imclone stock might be as follows:

"Sell to open, 5 Imclone August 45.00 Calls (QCIHI) at a limit of $5.50, for the day, all or none.

 "QCI is the symbol assigned to Imclone options. "H" indicates that it is an August Call. "I" gives us the price of $45.00

"This order would be filled when someone wants to buy 5 Imclone August 45.00 Calls for $5.50 or more. If the market has moved down when the order is placed it may not fill. If the market is moving up it could fill at $5.50 or even higher. If it is not filled before the end of the day it expires.

"A future order to close out this position could be as follows:

"Buy to close, 5 Imclone August 45.00 Calls (QCIHI) at the market for the day.

"This order would be filled at the next available ask price for the option. Since it is a market order the actual price for each of the 5 contracts may be different. Also it may be only partial filled."

"Professor, why would we want to buy to close an option?" asked Jake.

"This is an example of managing your accounts while you are waiting for the expiration date. A wise old investor was once asked what he thought the stock market would do. His response was: 'It will fluctuate.' And indeed it will. The stock on which you have sold a covered call will fluctuate in value. As the stock fluctuates so does the premium, or price of the call option. For example you expect to receive $5.50 a share for your call options on Imclone. In a few days or weeks that same option, QCIHI, may be trading for $5.00 or less. If you think the stock is going to come roaring back, bringing the value of the option with it, then "buy to close" at the lower price and sell again later at the higher premium.

"Okay, let's move on to some record keeping checklists I recommend. A disciplined approach is desirable in preparing an option order to prevent mistakes. Here are the steps I go through in preparing a trade:

1. Write down the trade that you intend to execute.

2. Get a quote on the stock and intended option. This will validate the option symbol, strike price, and strike month.

3. Calculate the return on each premium.

4. Determine if a market or limit order is appropriate.

5. Set the price on your order and then submit it.

"For example, you have 500 shares of ImClone in your account. You want to place an August covered call option trade and you do not want to have your stock called for less than $45.00 per share. Now you write down the option quotes you need to make a decision.

ImClone stock symbol is—IMCL

ImClone May $45.00 call symbol is—QCIEI

ImClone August $45.00 call symbol is—QCIHI

ImClone August $50.00 call symbol is—QCIHJ

You go to your quote provider (by phone or over the Internet) request the quote for each symbol and write it down."

Rob punched some numbers on the notepad. "Here is an earlier computation I had made on Imclone."

IMCL 45.20–45.28 Last trade 45.21 up .05

IMCL MAY 45.00 Call QCIEI 3.80-4.00

IMCL AUG 45.00 Call QCIHI 5.50-5.80

IMCL AUG 50.00 Call QCIHJ 3.50-3.80

"I've created a program I call the Call Option Wizard which computes gain, if called and if expired, for any combination of strike price and expiration date. It also compares the resulting percentages to my Magic Chart. Just to refresh your memory here is the formula we use to compute the gains."

$$\text{If Sold} = \frac{(\text{Strike Price} + \text{Premium} - \text{Purchase Price})}{\text{Purchase Price}}$$

$$\text{If Expired} = \frac{\text{Premium}}{\text{Purchase Price}}$$

"Here are the results based on a purchase price of $45.27."

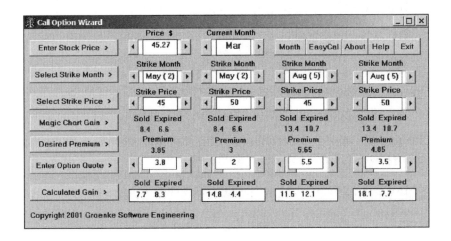

"You look at the Magic Chart table and determine which call option best fits *the money tree* model.

"Since ImClone is currently in an up trend you decide that a limit order at $5.50 should be filled within seconds.

"You write your order as follows:

"Sell 5 IMCL August 45 Calls to open at $5.50 for the day all or none.

"Now place your order and write its confirmation number on your order sheet.

"When your order is filled write out the detail of the order and the net proceeds of the action on your daily-completed order sheet. Save these sheets until you receive your confirmation from your broker. This is a precautionary measure only. If there are errors in the confirmation you need documentation to perform resolution. You will also need your daily trade results sheet to update your trading files and track your overall results.

"After I started trading options it became important to record and track each and every trade. I have done this since day one and now have the history of every trade I made in my blue file.

Why a blue file? For every trade you execute you will receive a trade confirmation in the mail from your broker. To keep these together and easily accessible I put them in a blue file folder instead of the standard cream colored ones. This allowed me to find this file very quickly since I was using it more and more each day. I also have a box on the daily order sheets, which gets checked indicating that the blue file was updated.

"In this blue file folder I have a transaction history tracking sheet on which I record my daily transactions such as, stock buys, call option sales, assignments, close outs, etc. I record the date, the transaction, and the net debit or credit for the trade. This is a running list and fills multiple pages for the year. After receiving the confirmation from the broker I use a highlighter and highlight the debit or credit on the tracking sheet to indicate that I received the trade confirmation and the results agree. The confirmations are filed in the order of the tracking sheet. This allows quick access if a reference is required. If a transaction is not highlighted within two weeks, I call the brokerage house and ask for a duplicate confirmation. It may not have been sent or it may have gotten lost in the mail. This process makes sure there is a paper trail for every transaction for tax or other purposes such as stockholder class action lawsuits. In the latter situation, you may be asked to provide copies of all transactions during a certain period to substantiate a possible claim and participate in any settlement. My greatest use of this record was the settlement on litigation regarding the NASDAQ market makers spread price fixing antitrust action. This is where the US Department of Justice brought a civil enforcement proceeding on July 17, 1996, alleging that twenty-four NASDAQ market makers, together with others, conspired to widen spreads in violation of the federal antitrust laws. To participate in this settlement, one had to supply detail records of related NASDAQ stock transactions for the defined period.

"The blue file contains all transactions in the order of execution by date. I also maintain a group of computer files called directory nineteen. In this directory I maintain a file by company of every transaction executed. From this directory I can extract every trade on any company that I have invested in and print out the trading history and corresponding overall gain or loss. I process this directory on a periodic basis to update my successful company list and to track overall results. I use the stock symbol as the file name, which prevents duplication while still being very informative. I backup this directory monthly and keep multiple backups for history and recovery if needed. All of the examples I've shown you are from this history file."

Jake raised his hand to ask a question and then with an embarrassed grin brought it back down. "Professor, I'm convinced this record keeping is important. But at this point I'm lost."

"Hmmm, yes I can understand this might be confusing. I developed it as I needed it and have been doing it so long it seems very simple to me. I have an idea. Why don't I put examples in the software program that you downloaded from my web site?[1] That should make your record keeping easy."

There was a buzz from someone downstairs wanting to come up. Jean excused herself.

Rob continued. "One other important record keeping requirement is a tax file. For taxes you need to actually move some cash from your brokerage account to a savings or money market account. This way you are not tempted to invest it. It is reserved for taxes so leave it there. You do not want to have to close out some calls and sell some stock in April to pay the taxes. It could be bad timing. Remember we are reserving for taxes because we plan to make money. It is one of the perks when you have gains. The amount to reserve depends on your tax bracket but here is good formula:

"Tax Reserve = (Total Option Premiums −Losses) x 25%"

"Speaking of taxes," Jean said jokingly as she returned with the visitor.

---

[1] KellerPublishing.com

Except for the long hair worn in a ponytail and the diamond stud in his left ear, the man looked like Rob Graham.

Rob rose with a smile and said, "Jake, Katie, I would like to introduce my twin brother, Greg. Greg these are our friends, Jake and Katie Kimball."

As hands were being shook Rob continued. "Greg is a distinguished professor of mathematics. He has been working on a formula that I think you will be interested in."

13

Take Action Indicator

Wealth is the product of man's capacity to think.
Ayn Rand

"Look at these incredible shells I found on Sand Dollar Island. And the birds. I can't get over it. You people actually live here. I'm just now beginning to relax. Soon I'll be back in the frozen north land."

Greg's New England pale skin had taken on a Marco Island tan in the week he had been visiting. Jean brought coffee for everyone and a slice of pie for Greg.

As the group settled back down Rob picked up his leather note pad. "Greg has developed a formula that I believe will be very valuable.

"Jake you know how important it is to pick the right stock. That's where I put my greatest emphasis. First build a qualified prospect list. Then qualify the list with Buy Limit and Buy Rank formulas. And finally you want to be sure the current price has crossed over the fifty day moving average."

"I'm with you up to this point," said Jake. "I've done all the homework although I haven't put it into practice yet."

Rob continued. "There are a lot of times when looking at a stock chart with a fifty-day moving average that I notice that the current price is below the Buy Limit and the fifty-day average. The stock is a prime prospect but the time for action is not quite here. How can I tell when it is time to act? I do not want to be too late but not too early either. I always felt there should be some way to combine the value of the Buy Rank with the fifty day moving average.

"I was inspired one evening when Jean and I were out walking and saw a shooting star, a small meteorite flashing across the earth's atmosphere. Some meteorites are reflected with a flash and others enter the atmosphere and display a burning tail as they near the earth. Why not develop a Take Action Indicator that signals when you should proceed with buying a stock and selling a covered call based on the current price approaching the buy limit and fifty-day moving average. As the price nears these values action should be taken. The challenge was putting the information into a formula that would give a reliable and consistent ranking.

"So when Greg came for a visit I knew he would soon be bored without a math challenge."

Greg smiled and sipped his coffee.

"Greg, why don't you explain it from here," said Rob as he handed over the note pad.

"I should explain that, thanks to brother Rob, I have been supplementing my teaching income for the past year with options trading. In the back of my mind was the thought that there should be something more definitive than the Buy Rank for taking action. But I hadn't actually made the conceptual leap until Rob explained the objective.

"There is an ideal situation and then next best. The ideal situation is when the buy rank is greater than five, the fifty-day average is flat or increasing, and the current price has just crossed the fifty day moving average.

"The next best is when the buy rank is positive and the current price is nearing or has just moved above the 50 day moving average. So here's the formula." Greg punched a few buttons on the note pad and the following formula appeared on the screen.

$$\text{TAI} = \frac{(CP)(CP) + 3(FDA)(BL - CP) - (BL)(CP)}{(CP)(L - BL) + 2(FDA)(BL - L)}$$

Greg continued as if it were the simplest thing in the world. "TAI stands for Take Action Indicator. CP is the current price of the stock that you are considering. FDA is the fifty-day moving average. BL is the Buy Limit and L is the fifty two week low."

With a look of utter despair Jake said, "Greg please. By the time I figure out this formula we'll be at the next expiration date."

"Oh," replied Greg in mock surprise. "Did you want the simple version? Well as a matter of fact I did get it a little simpler. In this one BR stands for Buy Rank."

$$TAI = BR \left(1 + \frac{FDA}{2(FDA) - CP} \right)$$

"Thanks Greg," said Rob. "I've tried it out and so far it works great. Remember when looking at the Buy Rank by itself, I said anytime it was positive it was good and above five it was great. The take action indicator is a little different. We want to take action when it is between 10 and −5, be cautious (wait) when it is between −5 and −10, and look at other opportunities if it is less than −10. If the TAI has a value above 10 it may still be okay to precede with this prospect but a second review of the fifty-two week price chart with the fifty-day moving average is in order to see if the stock is still in a downward trend. We may be too early so we want to verify it before we act.

"Here's what you are looking for on the TAI."

Rob wrote in his note pad and the following appeared on the screen.

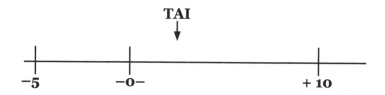

"Actually I can make it even easier for you. I have added a TAI column to the Prospect List Manager. Jake, that's the program you used to compute Buy Limit and Buy Rank for your prospect list. For each stock in your portfolio and prospect list you simply plug in the fifty two week low, fifty two week high and the fifty day moving average. The program computes Buy Limit, Buy Rank and TAI. You can sort the prospect list by any column. That makes it easy to decide which stock to add to your portfolio and which stocks in your portfolio you should sell."

Rob closed his note pad Illustrator and the screen became a live scene of a cabin on a lake in Minnesota. Ice cycles hung from the eves of the cabin and a cold rain was blowing across the frozen lake. Looking at Greg he said, "Does it make you homesick, brother?"

14

Simulation with Taxes and Losses

"One definition of an economist is somebody who sees something happen in practice and wonders if it will work in theory."
Ronald Reagan

The setting sun on the clear waters of the Caribbean was matched by the rising of a glorious full moon. Jake and Katie enjoyed the view as they walked across the top deck of the cruise ship where they were to meet Rob and Jean. Over the past year they had repeatedly sold calls on the 500 shares of Imclone stock, their first venture in the options market. With the Professor's assistance they had developed a portfolio of over thirty stocks which met their investment criteria and had a good yield in call premiums. Part of the monthly premium income was used for living expenses and the remainder was reinvested.

"Hurry, come look at the dolphins," Jean called to Jake and Katie from the port side of the deck. The dolphins seemed to be enjoying racing along with the fairly small luxury cruise ship. There were only 400 passengers and an equal number of staff and crew. The whole purpose of the cruise was the investment seminars sponsored by one of the major investment publications. Jake had written an article for the national magazine titled "The Professor's Money Tree" which resulted in Rob being invited to be one of the lecturers on the cruise.

"These are really posh accommodations," exclaimed Katie. "Now if I could just get these nautical terms right. Like how do you know which side is port and which side is starboard?"

The two couples enjoyed the beauty of the sky and the frolicking of the dolphins. Their destination was Grand Cayman. But the real purpose of the trip was to provide a pleasant setting for the financial seminars.

"I heard a bit of trivia once that helps me with those terms, port and starboard," said Rob. "And it has to do with the word 'posh' that you just used Katie. When cruise ships first started going out of London down the coast of Europe and through the straits of Gibraltar, the first class passengers wanted to be on the side of the ship with a view of the coast. Naturally they would be on the port or left side going down. Then on the return cruise home they would change to the staterooms on the right or starboard side of the ship so they would still have a view of the coast. The term 'port out starboard home' or simply posh, became synonymous with first class accommodations."

One of the staff came by with a tray of drinks and hors d'oeuvres. As they walked along the deck Jake commented to Rob, "You really got a lot of response last night on your lecture 'Make Your Own Dividends'. I could tell that was a real eye opener for most of the audience. What will you talk about in tonight's lecture?"

"You remember there was an important question asked the first night in the opening session that is typically not covered in these seminars. In fact the guy made the point that he had read a lot of books about making money in the stock market. All the systems he had read about never took into account that the market goes down as well as up, that you can and do have real losses in the stock market. I have developed a software program that simulates stock investments and the subsequent sell of covered calls. You can alter the various factors, including a stock loss, and see the resulting portfolio gain or loss over a period of time. My Illustrator works with the ships video system so I can run the simulation based on questions from the audience in real time."

"What about the Cedric Chart? Are you going to show that?" Jake had been amazed at the apparent accuracy of the Buy/Sell time line chart of unknown origin, perhaps made as early as the Civil War.

"Hmmm. The fat years, the lean years. It might be interesting to get the reaction of this sophisticated group of investors."

Their conversation was interrupted by the familiar ship's bell that indicated the captain was about to make an announcement.

"This is the Captain speaking. Tonight's lecture by Dr. Robert Graham has been moved to the Main Theater to facilitate the increased demand. Dr. Neal Dobbs's lecture on *Selecting the Right Mutual Fund* will now be held in Stateroom B."

*****

Three seats had been reserved on the front row for Jake, Katie and Jean. Rob walked immediately onto the stage and was introduced by the MC, Kudlow P. Cramer.

"Ladies and Gentlemen. Professor Graham will speak tonight on the subject 'Simulate Your Trading Plan'. As you know, last night's topic, 'Create Your Own Dividends', has been the main topic of conversation all day. I'm sure that accounts for the overflow crowd tonight."

A murmur went through the audience. "Yes, yes," the moderator continued. "I know some of you found last night's topic to be a little controversial, especially those of you associated with old line full service brokerage houses." As most of the audience laughed, recalling the professor's blunt talk about the individual investor's ability to manage his own investment account, Kudlow winked at Rob. Rob smiled in return but otherwise maintained a professional decorum.

"Please welcome once again Professor Robert Graham."

The standing ovation surprised Rob. He quickly motioned for the audience to be seated so he could begin his presentation.

"Before I initiate a trade I simulate its effect on my portfolio for the next three years out. If I am selling a call on a stock I own, I want to know the effect of tying up the underlying value of the long stock position. If I write a six-month call option I know that the stock is committed and the plan is that it will be called. If it is called the cash received for the underlying stock value is used to buy a new position from my prospect list and again write covered calls. If the stock is not called I need to make a basic decision. I will either liquidate my position in the stock because of changes in the company and the marketplace or I sell a new call option. Selling a new call option requires a decision as to the new strike price and months to expiration. On some of my stocks I have sold covered calls over a dozen times. As one three month or six month call option expires I sell a new one. That generates a powerful compounding effect.

"All of these factors can be easily simulated in a program I have developed for just this purpose.

"Last night I talked to you about creating dividends on stocks that don't pay dividends. That's the money tree effect: generating income by selling covered calls. It's nice to have an orchard of money trees. Each month you can pluck some fruit from some of the trees in your orchard.

"But . . ." Rob paused to be sure he had everyone's full attention. "But suppose some of the trees go bad. By that I mean suppose some of the stocks you select in your portfolio go down in value. What effect will that have on our plan to generate a high rate of return on our investment? That's the purpose of the simulation. We want to gain confidence that we can generate a high return even if some of our stocks go bad.

"It is important to set down a goal. In most cases option values follow the normal ups and downs of the market, so let's be realistic in our expected gains. Is 20% possible? Yes. Is 30% possible? Yes. Is 50% possible? Yes, a 50% gain in one year on your investments with options is possible because I've been there, done that! Okay, what is realistic? Let's pick a goal of 25%. Would you agree that a 25% return on your stock portfolio would be pretty good?

"Here is the plan. We'll keep it simple for illustration purposes. We are going to take $25000 and buy three different stocks and sell covered calls. I like to have income coming in each month so for the first month I will sell a one month call on one stock, a two month call on the second stock and a three month call on the third stock. We'll assume we are starting in January. In February and subsequent months we will sell three month calls.

"We start the simulation with an initial investment of $25000."

Rob punched the number into his Illustrator and it flashed on the three large screens, one directly in front of the audience and two on each side. "We need to make a couple of assumptions. First how much premium as a percentage of the stock price could you expect to get for a three month option? My experience has been that you can fairly easily get 10% return for three months. You will need to test this yourself by checking the call premiums on some of your favorite stocks. You should easily get this information from your online broker. Or go to www.wallstreetcity.com You may find it easier to get, say, 4% for one month than 10% for three months. It all depends on stock volatility. The higher the volatility the greater the premium. Anyway for our simulation we will use 3.3% a month or 10% for three months.

"Now the next assumption is stock loss. Unless you are absolutely brilliant and extremely lucky, you will pick some stocks that insist on going down in value rather than up. I will use a 15% loss factor. The simulator will sell two of my stocks each year for a combined loss of 15% of the beginning of year portfolio value. Does that seem reasonable?"

There were murmurs of agreement through out the room.

"Now there is one other factor we need to consider. What about taxes? At the end of each year I will have the simulation deduct 25% of the net income—call premiums less stock losses—from the portfolio to keep the tax man happy. For simplicity I have ignored commission expense and gains from stock appreciation. Commissions are low if you use a good online broker and would be more than off set by gains from stock appreciation. Also in this particular simulation we are not using the leverage available in margin accounts."

SIMULATION SETUP SUMMARY
PORTFOLIO GROWTH THROUGH
SELL OF COVERED CALLS

FACTORS:

1. INITIAL INVESTMENT: $25,000

2. 10% PREMIUM PER QUARTER
   (3.3% PER MONTH)

3. ASSUMED STOCK LOSSES EACH YEAR OF 15% OF
   BEGINNING BALANCE

4. ASSUMED TAX OF 25% OF NET INCOME (PREMIUMS
   LESS LOSSES)

As Rob finished punching numbers in the Illustrator the following was shown on the screen:

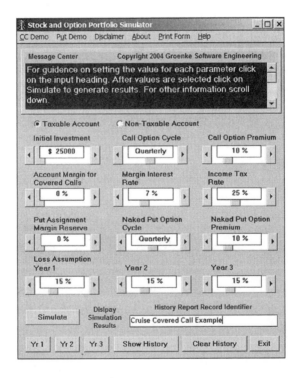

"OK. Are you ready? Here comes the simulation for the first six months."

YEAR ONE

MONTH	TRANSACTION	AMT	BAL	INC
JAN	INITIAL INVESTMENT BUY A & SELL MAR CALLS OPTIONS SOLD AT 6.7 % BUY B & SELL APR CALLS OPTIONS SOLD AT 10 % BUY C & SELL FEB CALLS OPTIONS SOLD AT 3.3 % OPTION PREM INCOME JAN	25000 −12500 837 −10670 1067 − 3734 123	25000 12500 13337 2667 3734 -0- 123	2027
FEB	STK C CALLED OR EXPIRED STK C SELL MAY CALLS OPTIONS SOLD AT 10 % OPTION PREM INCOME FEB	3734 − 3857 385	3857 -0- 385	385
MAR	STK A CALLED OR EXPIRED STK A SELL JUN CALLS OPTIONS SOLD AT 10 % OPTION PREM INCOME MAR	12500 12885 1288	12885 -0- 1288	1288
APR	STK B CALLED OR EXPIRED STK B SELL JUL CALLS OPTIONS SOLD AT 10 % OPTION PREM INCOME APR	10670 11958 1195	11958 -0- 1195	1195
MAY	STK C CALLED OR EXPIRED STK C SELL AUG CALLS OPTIONS SOLD AT 10 % OPTION PREM INCOME MAY	3857 −5053 505	5053 -0- 505	505
JUNE	STK A CALLED OR EXPIRED STK A SELL SEP CALLS OPTIONS SOLD AT 10 % OPTION PREM INCOME JUN	12885 -13391 1339	13391 -0- 1339	1339

"Let's go over this first six months and I think you will quickly get the hang of it. In January we make an initial investment in our brokerage account of $25,000. We buy three stocks, A, B & C, carefully selected from our prospect list. You recall last night I talked briefly about my system of ranking stocks and use of the TAI formula. Stock selection is very important but for tonight's discussion we are focusing on the three year simulation.

"For our first purchase of stock A we sell March calls for a premium of 6.7%. For simplicity we are assuming the strike price is the same as the purchase price when in reality the strike price would frequently be about 5 to 10% above the purchase price.

"The premium received of $837 is added to our account balance and used in the purchase of stocks B & C. Thus the compounding effect begins the very first month. On stock B we sell April calls and on stock C we sell February calls. In subsequent months all calls will be for three months. By staggering the calls the first month and then selling three month options we are able to have premium income each month.

"Each stock will either be called, in which case we receive cash, or the option will expire. Either event leaves us in position to repeat the process, selling additional calls and reinvesting at least part of the premium received.

"Now let's take a look at the last six months and portfolio value at year end."

MONTH	TRANSACTION	AMT	BAL	INC
JULY	STK B CALLED OR EXPIRED	11958	13297	
	STK B SELL OCT CALLS	-13297	-0-	
	OPTIONS SOLD AT 10 %	1329	1329	
	OPTION PREM INCOME JUL			1329
AUG	STK C CALLED OR EXPIRED	5053	6383	
	STK C SELL NOV CALLS	-6383	-0-	
	OPTIONS SOLD AT 10 %	638	638	
	OPTION PREM INCOME AUG			638
SEP	STK A SOLD AT LOSS			
	(13391 – 1500)	11891	12529	
	NEW A SELL DEC CALLS	-10023	2505	
	OPTIONS SOLD AT 10 %	1002	3508	
	BUY D SELL DEC CALLS	-3508	-0-	
	OPTIONS SOLD AT 10 %	350	350	
	OPTION PREM INCOME SEP			1353
OCT	STK B SOLD AT LOSS			
	(13297 – 2250)	11047	11398	
	NEW B SELL JAN CALLS	-11398	-0-	
	OPTIONS SOLD AT 10 %	1139	1139	
	OPTION PREM INCOME OCT			1139
NOV	STK C CALLED OR EXPIRED	6383	7523	
	STK C SELL FEB CALLS	-7523	-0-	
	OPTIONS SOLD AT 10 %	752	752	
	OPTION PREM INCOME NOV			752
DEC	A&D CALLED OR EXPIRED	13531	14284	
	STK A&D SELL MAR CALLS	-14284	-0-	
	OPTIONS SOLD AT 10 %	1428	1428	
	TAX RESERVE	-2408	-980	
	OPTION PREM INCOME DEC			1428
TOTAL PREMIUM INCOME YEAR ONE				**13378**

PORTFOLIO VALUE AT YEAR END		
		BALANCE
STOCK A & D	14284	14284
STOCK B	11398	25682
STOCK C	7523	33205
CASH (DEC PREMIUMS)	1428	34633
25% TAX ON NET INCOME (PREMIUMS LESS LOSSES)	-2408	**32225**
ASSUMED STOCK LOSSES		3750
GAIN AFTER TAX & LOSS		7225
RETURN ON INVESTMENT		28.90%

"Notice the transactions in September and October. In those months we incur stock market losses of $1500 and $2250, 15% of the beginning of year portfolio balance. These losses reflect real life experiences. No matter how careful you are there will be stock market losses. For simulation purposes we have just assumed we will lose 15% each year. These losses could occur because the stock price went down and we decided to sell the stock. Perhaps the stock no longer meets our stock selection criteria such as profitable quarters or volume of trades. Another way we could have a loss is when the market price goes down and we decide to sell calls at a lower strike price than our original purchase price. If that happens and the stock is called we again have a stock loss. In that case the loss may well be offset by premium income, but it is still a loss. A stock market strategy is only worthwhile if it can overcome those losses and still show a significant gain.

"Notice in December we deduct $2,408 for tax reserve. This is 25% of net income, $13,378 premium income less the $3,750 stock losses. Taxes are even more certain than stock market losses. It's best to just accept the fact that you are going to make money and you will need to pay taxes. As the quantity of premium income increases you will probably need to make quarterly payments to the IRS. Plan ahead. Set aside a reserve for taxes so you aren't caught in a situation of having to liquidate some investments to pay taxes.

"Finally, how did we do for the year? Even after taxes and market losses our portfolio value has grown to $32,225, all from the sale of call options. We are ignoring the possibility of stock market appreciation.

"Our portfolio growth of $7,225 represents a return on investment of 28.9%. Let's move on to year two."

Rob flashed all of year two and the summary onto the screens.

YEAR TWO

MONTH	TRANSACTION	AMT	BAL	INC
JAN	BALANCE FORWARD		-980	
	STK B CALLED OR EXPIRED	11398	10418	
	STK B SELL APR CALLS	-10418	-0-	
	OPTIONS SOLD AT 10 %	1041	1041	
	OPTION PREM INCOME JAN			1041
FEB	STK C CALLED OR EXPIRED	7523	8565	
	STK C SELL MAY CALLS	- 8565	-0-	
	OPTIONS SOLD AT 10 %	856	856	
	OPTION PREM INCOME FEB			856
MAR	A&D CALLED OR EXPIRED	14284	15140	
	STK A SELL JUN CALLS	7570	7570	
	OPTIONS SOLD AT 10 %	757	8327	
	STK D SELL JUN CALLS	8327	-0-	
	OPTIONS SOLD AT 10 %	833	833	
	OPTION PREM INCOME MAR			1590
APR	STK B SOLD AT A LOSS (10418 – 1450)	8968	9801	
	STK B SELL JUL CALLS	-9801	-0-	
	OPTIONS SOLD AT 10 %	980	980	
	OPTION PREM INCOME APR			980

(continued next page)

MONTH	TRANSACTION	AMT	BAL	INC
MAY	STK C CALLED OR EXPIRED STK C SELL AUG CALLS OPTIONS SOLD AT 10 % OPTION PREM INCOME MAY	8565 -9545 954	9545 -0- 954	 954
JUNE	A & D CALLED OR EXPIRED STK A SELL SEP CALLS OPTIONS SOLD AT 10 % STK D SELL SEP CALLS OPTIONS SOLD AT 10 % OPTION PREM INCOME JUNE	15897 -8426 843 -9269 927	16852 8426 9269 -0- 927	 1770
JULY	STK B CALLED OR EXPIRED STK B SELL OCT CALLS OPTIONS SOLD AT 10 % OPTION PREM INCOME JUL	9801 -10728 1072	10728 -0- 1072	 1072
AUG	STK C CALLED OR EXPIRED STK C SELL NOV CALLS OPTIONS SOLD AT 10 % OPTION PREM INCOME AUG	9545 -10617 1062	10617 -0- 1062	 1062
SEP	A&D CALLED OR EXPIRED NEW A SELL DEC CALLS OPTIONS SOLD AT 10 % NEW D SELL DEC CALLS OPTIONS SOLD AT 10 % OPTION PREM INCOME SEP	17695 9378 938 10316 1031	18757 9378 10316 -0- 1031	 1969
OCT	STK B CALLED OR EXPIRED STK B SELL JAN CALLS OPTIONS SOLD AT 10 % OPTION PREM INCOME OCT	10728 11759 1176	11759 -0- 1176	 1176
NOV	STK C SOLD AT A LOSS (10617 - 3384) STK C SELL FEB CALLS OPTIONS SOLD AT 10 % OPTION PREM INCOME NOV	 7234 -8410 841	 8410 -0- 841	 841
DEC	A&D CALLED OR EXPIRED NEW A SELL MAR CALLS OPTIONS SOLD AT 10 % NEW D SELL MAR CALLS OPTIONS SOLD AT 10 % TAX RESERVE OPTION PREM INCOME DEC	19694 10268 1027 11294 1129 2659	20535 10267 11294 -0- 1129 -1530	 2156
TOTAL PREMIUM INCOME YEAR TWO			**15467**	

PORTFOLIO VALUE AT YEAR END		
		BALANCE
STOCK A	10268	10268
STOCK B	11759	22027
STOCK C	8410	30437
STOCK D	11295	41732
CASH	1129	42861
25% TAX ON NET INCOME (PREMIUMS LESS LOSSES)	-2659	**40202**
ASSUMED STOCK LOSSES		4834
GAIN AFTER TAX & LOSS		7977
RETURN ON INVESTMENT		24.75%

"The key point here," Rob began, "is that the advantages of compounding are powerful but begin slowly. Our portfolio has grown by almost $8,000 or 24.75%. Accordingly we have larger stock losses and reserve for taxes.

"Let's go on to year three."

YEAR THREE

MONTH	TRANSACTION	AMT	BAL	INC
JAN	BALANCE FORWARD B CALLED OR EXPIRED STK B SELL APR CALLS OPTIONS SOLD AT 10 % OPTION PREM INCOME APR	 11759 -10229 1023	-1530 10229 -0- 1023	 1023
FEB	STK C CALLED OR EXPIRED STK C SELL MAY CALLS OPTIONS SOLD AT 10 % OPTION PREM INCOME FEB	8410 - 9433 943	9433 -0- 943	 943
MAR	A&D CALLED OR EXPIRED STK A SELL JUN CALLS OPTIONS SOLD AT 10 % STK D SELL JUN CALLS OPTIONS SOLD AT 10 % NEW E SELL JUN CALLS OPTIONS SOLD AT 10 % OPTION PREM INCOME MAR	21562 11253 1125 -9902 990 -3465 346	22505 11252 12377 2475 3465 -0- 346	 2462
APR	STK B CALLED OR EXPIRED STK B SELL JUL CALLS OPTIONS SOLD AT 10 % OPTION PREM INCOME APR	10230 -10576 1057	10576 -0- 1057	 1057
MAY	STK C CALLED OR EXPIRED STK C SELL AUG CALLS OPTIONS SOLD AT 10 % OPTION PREM INCOME MAY	9433 -10490 1049	10490 -0- 1049	 1049
JUNE	A&D CALLED OR EXPIRED STK A SELL SEP CALLS OPTIONS SOLD AT 10 % STK D SELL SEP CALLS OPTIONS SOLD AT 10 % STK E SELL SEP CALLS OPTIONS SOLD AT 10 % OPTION PREM INCOME JUN	24621 -12835 1283 -11295 1129 -3953 395	25670 12835 14118 2824 3953 -0- 395	 2808

MONTH	TRANSACTION	AMT	BAL	INC
JULY	STK B SOLD AT LOSS (10756 – 3015) NEW B SELL OCT CALLS OPTIONS SOLD AT 10 % OPTION PREM INCOME JUL	7561 -7956 795	7956 -0- 795	 795
AUG	STK C CALLED OR EXPIRED STK C SELL NOV CALLS OPTIONS SOLD AT 10 % OPTION PREM INCOME AUG	10491 -11286 1128	11286 -0- 1128	 1128
SEP	STK D SOLD AT LOSS (11295 – 3015) NEW D SELL DEC CALLS OPTIONS SOLD AT 10 % A&E CALLED OR EXPIRED STK A SELL DEC CALLS OPTIONS SOLD AT 10 % STK E SELL DEC CALLS OPTIONS SOLD AT 10 % NEW F SELL DEC CALLS OPTIONS SOLD AT 10 % OPTION PREM INCOME SEP	8280 -6706 670 16788 -10478 1048 -8584 858 -3004 300	9408 2702 3372 20160 9682 10730 2146 3004 -0- 300	 2876
OCT	STK B CALLEDOR EXPIRED STK B SELL JAN CALLS OPTIONS SOLD AT 10 % OPTION PREM INCOME OCT	7957 -8257 826	8257 -0- 826	 826
NOV	STK C CALLEDOR EXPIRED STK C SELL FEB CALLS OPTIONS SOLD AT 10 % OPTION PREM INCOME NOV	11286 -12112 1211	12112 -0- 1211	 1211
DEC	A,D,E&F CALLED NEW A SELL MAR CALLS OPTIONS SOLD AT 10 % NEW D SELL MAR CALLS OPTIONS SOLD AT 10 % STK E SELL MAR CALLS OPTIONS SOLD AT 10 % STK F SELL MAR CALLS OPTIONS SOLD AT 10 % TAX RESERVE OPTION PREM INCOME DEC	28773 -11994 1199 -7676 768 -9825 982 -3438 343 3361	29984 17990 19190 11514 12282 2456 3438 -0- 343 –3018	 3292
TOTAL PREMIUM INCOME YEAR THREE				**19470**

PORTFOLIO VALUE AT YEAR END		
		BALANCE
STOCK A	11994	11994
STOCK B	8257	20251
STOCK C	12112	32363
STOCK D	7676	40039
STOCK E	9825	49864
STOCK F	3438	53302
CASH	343	53645
25% TAX ON NET INCOME (PREMIUMS LESS LOSSES)	-3361	**50284**
ASSUMED STOCK LOSSES		6030
GAIN AFTER TAX & LOSS		10082
RETURN ON INVESTMENT		25.07%

"Here we are at the end of year three. As the portfolio has grown we have diversified. We began with only three stocks and now have six. Of course, in real life, further diversification is possible and desirable.

"In three years we have doubled our portfolio from $25,000 to $50,000. The compounding effect is just beginning to take effect. In another three years the portfolio can grow to $100,000. After 10 years we could grow the $25,000 to $250,000 based on our assumptions of 10% premium for three months, 25% tax and 15% stock market losses."

Kudlow P. Cramer, the host and moderator, walked back on stage and shook hands with Rob as the audience burst into an appreciative round of applause.

"Professor, I have a few questions from the audience if you don't mind."

Rob nodded agreement.

"Question one: For self directed IRA's and other retirement plans on which taxes are deferred, what would be the simulated result without taxes?"

Rob quickly punched some numbers on his Illustrator and the following table flashed on the screen.

"I have run the simulation with different factors. If you avoid tax, as with a retirement account, and all other factors are the same as the simulation we just demonstrated, then the $25,000 grows to $61,540 in three years. Here are some interesting scenarios, beginning with the one demonstrated in detail tonight.

"The premium percentage is the call option premium divided by its underlying stock cost for the cycle indicated. For the last three simulations using funds borrowed from the brokerage account an interest rate of 7% is factored in as an expense."

COVERED CALL SIMULATION RESULTS						
Initial Invest.	Prem.	Cycle	Margin	Loss	Tax	3 YR Result
$25,000	10%	Quarterly	-0-	15%	25%	$50,284
$25,000	10%	Quarterly	-0-	15%	-0-	$61,540
$25,000	3%	Monthly	-0-	15%	-0-	$49,507
$25,000	4%	Monthly	40%	15%	25%	$73,406
$25,000	8%	Quarterly	40%	15%	25%	$48,965
$25,000	10%	Quarterly	40%	15%	25%	$62,861

"Next question: what about puts? The simulation only used covered calls."

"In my personal portfolio I use a strategy that combines both calls and puts to optimize return. For the beginning options investor I strongly recommend sticking with covered calls until you have gained experience.

"The simulation model allows you to include a certain level of put activity along with your covered calls. If we allow for example 40% of our margin to be used to cover the addition of naked puts to the previous simulation the account balance after three years is $71,617 instead of the $50,284 shown. This additional gain is from selling puts and using the premium to invest in more covered calls.

"There are many combinations of calls and puts that one can consider. That is why the Stock and Option Portfolio Simulation software module is one of the most valuable tools to own since it makes all those what ifs understandable."

"Professor Graham, this has been a very illuminating presentation. We have one final question. Are you a bull or a bear with respect to the next few years?"

Rob smiled. This was a question he could always expect. "I recently came across a chart that this group might find interesting. It's called 'Historical Buy & Sell Time Line' and goes from 1850 to 2018. I've been referring to it as the Cedric Chart because I learned about it from a newspaper column by Cedric Adams, a famous Minnesota newspaper columnist and radio personality very popular in the 1950s. Let's see if I can pull it up and flash it on the screen.

"Ah, here we go. I will leave it to you to decide the predictive value of the chart. I have personally been impressed with how 'right on' the chart has been in prior years. If it is accurate we are in for a few fat years. But lookout for the dip after 2007."

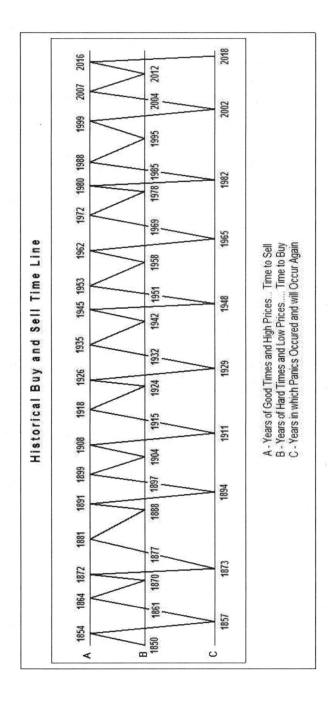

Cedric's Chart

Historical Buy and Sell Time Line

A - Years of Good Times and High Prices... Time to Sell
B - Years of Hard Times and Low Prices..... Time to Buy
C - Years in which Panics Occured and will Occur Again

Kudlow Cramer again broke in. "We have run out of time for additional questions. Thanks Rob for the wonderful insights into taking investment matters into our own hands. Maybe I can get you to visit me on my TV show. I know you would be an exciting guest. If anyone else has a question for Rob and does not get it answered before the end of the cruise, he has agreed to accept questions at <u>robgrahamphd@aol.com</u>."

*****

Later that evening Jake and Katie invited Rob and Jean to join them on the balcony of their stateroom. Katie brought out mugs of decaf as they enjoyed the view of the full moon glistening on the Caribbean and reflected on the events of the past year.

Finally Jake broached a subject that had been on his mind lately. "Professor, the buzz about the Cedric Chart was really interesting. I didn't think we would ever get out of the auditorium there were so many questions. I wonder if there is actually something to it. If the market follows definite patterns would it be possible to model the market?"

Rob smiled, gazing at the full moon. "I've done it!"

Jake noticed that Katie and Jean were engrossed in their own conversation. He noticed the taste of the coffee and he noticed a meteor cross the sky. And in a moment of self reflection he realized he wasn't really aware of any of those events. His mind was focused on the professor's last comment. "I've done it."

15

Modeling the Market

Money, which represents the prose of life, and which is
hardly spoken of in parlors without an apology, is, in
its effects and laws, as beautiful as roses.
Ralph Waldo Emerson

The next morning Jake and Rob were playing a game of chess in the ship's library. Jake, playing the white pieces, decided to ignore convention and fianchettoed both bishops. Rob quickly took command of the center. Kibitzers were gathering on both sides. Their focused attention was broken by the familiar chime of the captain's bell.

"Please pardon the interruption," the Captain began. "Special announcement concerning lectures. The Cedric Chart presented by Professor Rob Graham last evening has created so much interest that there will be a special presentation this afternoon at 2:00 PM. I am told by our investment host, Kudlow P. Cramer, that the professor will be explaining his software program which models the market."

At 2:00 PM the auditorium was again packed.

Cramer quickly introduced Rob and activated his lavaliere microphone.

"I am sure you have found the Cedric Chart interesting. The area of simulation and forecasting has always interested me. Lots of people have said they would like to see more detail on what the future may hold. So I took on the challenge and completed a stock market simulation model that tries to provide additional detail for various stocks and indexes.

"Some people say look at the past and use it to predict the future.

Others say it is completely random and the past has no bearing. A little of both is needed.

"There are only three possibilities for the market each day. It will go up, down, or stay the same. It is like the toss of a coin. The results will be heads or tails. Very seldom will it land on its edge. All major indexes change each day. Again very seldom has a major market index stayed exactly the same from one day to the next. It is safe to say then that the probability that the market will go up tomorrow is 50% and that it will go down is 50%. The big question is how much will it go up or down. Here one needs to apply some statistical analysis and forecasting.

"History will show us what the largest daily loss and gain were. The probability that tomorrow's change will fall in this high/low range of the last year is very high. Likely better than 99%. But again the question is how much will the market change tomorrow.

"If you do an analysis of the daily price change of any major index you will see that it follows a bell curve. Here is such a curve for the NASDAQ for 2002.

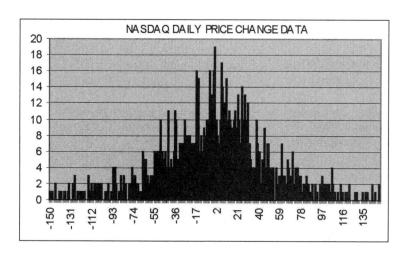

"What you see is the frequency (y-axes) that the NASDAQ went up or down one, two, three, etc. points during 2002. This data will vary by stock and index since each is changing on its own cycle and price curve.

"Let's take two jars and place all daily up price changes in one jar, and all down price changes in the other. This will provide us with a source for realistic daily price changes.

"We now can determine if the market will go up or down (toss a coin) and how much the price will change from our daily price change jar. We have everything we need to build a model and forecast any index or stock. Or do we? There is one thing missing and that is the general direction or trend of the index or stock. Here is where one needs to add some intelligence as to what may be expected.

"There are many market forces at work. Direction of interest rates, unemployment rate, price of oil, GDP Growth rate, strength of the US dollar, the current year of The U.S. Presidential cycle, consumer sentiment, earnings and revenue growth, surprise analyst upgrade or downgrade, surprise earnings up or down announcements, etc. There also are general market forecasts by economists, ratings such as the Standards and Poor one to five stars, or simple guides as given by the Cedric Chart.

"I have selected a set of these factors and come up with a composite, which I am calling the Rob Graham Factor or RG factor for short.

"The RG Factor can be neutral, positive, or negative. We apply the factor to the probability that tomorrow will be up or down. For example, if the factor is positive we change the probability that tomorrow will be an up day a number of times during the year and the trend should be up. This is like changing the coin so that if heads indicates an up day, we will toss more heads than tails. If the factor is negative we change the probability to more down days.

"We have all the parameters for our model and now are ready to make a forecast of let's say the NASDAQ market.

"We start by flipping our special RG Factor weighted coin for up or down and randomly pick a price change from the up or down jar and add it to the NASDAQ yearend closing price. This gives us the closing price for day one. Now we repeat this for all the trading days in the period and we have a forecast. Seems a little tedious so why not take our PC and add a little software engineering and create a simulation model to simulate the task.

"What I have created is a Stock Market Simulator. By definition a simulator is a laboratory device that enables the operator to reproduce under test conditions phenomena likely to occur in actual performance. Hopefully the Stock Market Simulator will live up to this definition.

"Here are simulation results from The Money Tree Stock Market Simulator for 2003-04 for the NASDAQ, DOW30, and S&P 500 indexes.

"The factors used in this simulation for 2003-04 were as follows:

		2003	*2004*
1.	Interest rates	Down	Up
2.	Unemployment rate	Up	Down
3.	Price of oil	Flat	Up
4.	GDP growth	Up	Up
5.	U.S. dollar	Flat	Weaker
6.	Presidential year	Third	Fourth
7.	Cedric Chart view	C to A	C to A

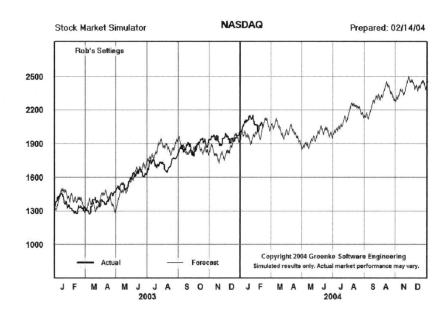

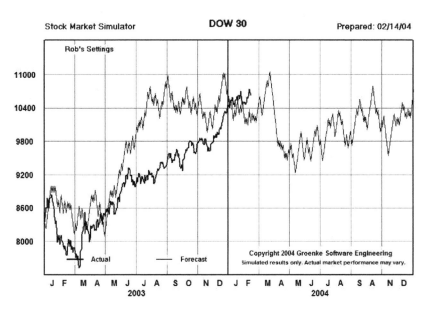

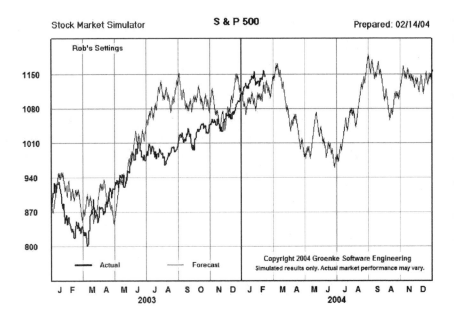

"You will notice that I have also included the actual results for the year for comparison. I let the charts speak for themselves.

"Now what about a little further out? Let's setup the simulation for 2003 through 2006 on the input form as follows:

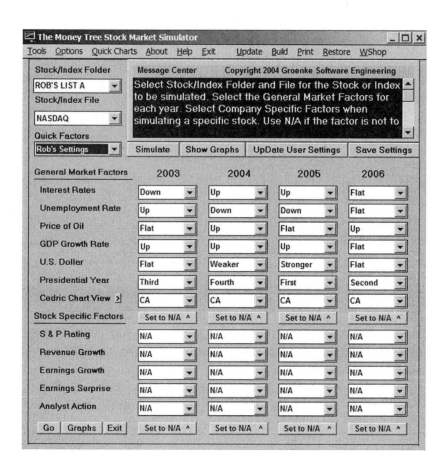

"After we select the NASDAQ index and set the Quick Factors to Rob's Settings we click Simulate and then Show Graphs. The graph for 2003 to 2006 is now displayed as follows:

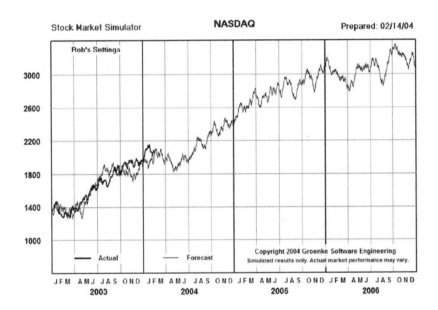

"You have been very attentive. Thank you. That concludes my presentation."

The appreciative applause continued as Kudlow P. Kramer joined Rob on stage and thanked him for the presentation.

"Rob, I know I speak for everyone here in saying how much we have learned from all three of your presentations. The first night you explained your strategy of creating dividends by selling options and you covered your formulas for computing Buy Limit and Buy Rank." Kudlow was consulting his notes. "And I was particularly impressed with your Magic Chart for deciding the optimum option premium. And of course last night you simulated a $25,000 portfolio used to sell covered calls over a three year period. Tonight's presentation of your Stock Market Simulation was also very enlightening.

"There is one question I am sure is on everyone's mind. And that is, How can we obtain a copy of your software programs?"

Rob smiled. "I've decided to make my software programs available to the public for a modest fee. Demonstration software can be downloaded for free. I'll put on the screen the programs I now have available. You can download them from my web site KellerPublishing.com or request a CD by mail."

The following chart appeared on the screen.

Professor Rob Graham Software Programs
THE MONEY TREE SOFTWARE TOOLS FOR WRITING COVERED CALLS AND NAKED PUTS ($ 24.95) *INCLUDES: THE CALL & PUT OPTIONS SIMULATOR, PROSPECT LIST MANAGER, BUY/LIMIT & BUY/RANK WIZARD, CALL OPTION WIZARD, PUT OPTION WIZARD, TRAINING WORKSHOP*
THE MONEY TREE STOCK MARKET SIMULATOR ($ 69.95) *INCLUDES FORECAST FOR 8 INDEXES AND OPTION TO ADD 128 ADDITIONAL STOCKS OR INDEXES*
EXCEL WORKSHEETS ($ 19.95) *INCLUDES A PROSPECT LIST TEMPLATE, OPTION PLAN TEMPLATE, AND STOCK TRANSACTION AND HISTORY TEMPLATE*
SPECIAL OFFER—ALL THREE ITEMS ABOVE ($89.95)

That evening Jake and Katie were guests of Rob and Jean on their balcony. The two couples toasted each other on a most satisfying cruise and enjoyed the warm ambience.

During a lull in the conversations Jake commented, "Did you notice how interested the audience was in factors controlling the market. They seemed eager to learn more after their small exposure to your market model and simulator."

"Yes," Rob replied. "I've actually been thinking the same thing. By the way how is your Great American Novel coming?"

Jake shrugged his shoulders and managed a negative grunt.

"As time passes I'm becoming more and more confidant in the predictive value of my market model. Maybe we should collaborate on a book about modeling the market," Rob continued.

"Something to think about," said Jake. "I have certainly benefited from all your software tools.We're planning an Alaska cruise next month."

GLOSSARY

American Stock Exchange (AMEX) A private, not-for-profit corporation, located in New York City, that handles approximately one-fifth of all securities trades within the United States.

American Style Option An option contract that can be exercised at any time between the date of purchase and the expiration date. The other type of contract is the European Style which may be exercised only during a specified period of time just prior to its expiration. Most exchange-traded options are American style.

Arbitrage The simultaneous purchase and sale of identical financial instruments in order to make a profit where the selling price is higher than the buying price.

Arbitrageur An individual that takes advantage of momentary disparities in prices between markets which enables one to lock in profits because the selling price is higher than the buying price.

Ask Price The current cost to buy a security or option. It is the lowest price the seller will accept at that time.

At-The-Money When an option's strike price is the same as the price of the underlying stock.

Automatic Exercise The automatic exercise of an option that is in-the-money on expiration date.

Bear An investor whose sentiment or belief is that a security or the market is falling or is expected to fall.

Bear Call Spread A strategy in which a trader sells a lower strike call and buys a higher strike call to create a trade with limited profit and limited risk. A fall in the price of the underlying stock increases the value of the spread. This is a net credit (cash inflow) transaction. The maximum loss is the difference between the strike prices less the credit. The maximum gain equals the credit.

Bear Market   The stock market cycle where prices for the overall market fall for an extended period of time usually caused by a weak economy and subsequent decreased corporate profits. It is generally agreed that a bear market is when the stock market experiences a price decline of twenty percent or more, and lasts at least two months.

Bear Put Spread   A strategy in which a trader sells a lower strike put and buys a higher strike put to create a trade with limited profit and limited risk. A fall in the price of the underlying stock increases the value of the spread. This is a net debit (cash outflow) transaction. The maximum gain is the difference between the strike prices less the debit. The maximum loss is equal to the debit.

Bid Price   The current price you would receive if a stock (or option) is sold. It is the highest price the buyer will pay for that security at the present time.

Black Scholes Formula   A pricing model that is used by most options exchanges to price various options. It factors in the current stock price, strike price, time until expiration, current interest rates, and volatility of the underlying security.

Break-even   The price of an underlying security at which an option strategy neither gains nor loses money.

Bull   An investor whose sentiment or belief is that a security or the market is rising or is expected to rise.

Bull Market   The stock market cycle where prices for the overall market rise for an extended period of time usually caused by a strong economy and subsequent increased corporate profits.

Bull Call Spread   A strategy in which a trader buys a lower strike call and sells a higher strike call to create a trade with limited profit and limited risk. A rise in the price of the underlying stock increases the value of the spread. This is a net debit (cash outflow) transaction. The maximum loss is equal to the initial debit. The maximum gain is the difference between the strike prices less the debit.

Bull Put Spread A strategy in which a trader sells a higher strike put and buys a lower strike put to create a trade with limited profit and limited risk. A rise in the price of the underlying stock increases the value of the spread. This is a net credit (cash inflow) transaction. The maximum loss is the difference between the strike prices less credit. The maximum gain is equal to the credit.

Buy Limit The maximum price that should ever be paid for a stock, based on its 52 week low (L) and 52 week high (H).

$$\text{Buy Limit} = L + .25\,(H-L)$$

Buy Rank A formula to rank the relative appeal of stocks on the prospect list. In the formula BL is Buy Limit, CP is current price, H is the 52 week high and L is the 52 week low.

$$\text{Buy Rank} = \frac{10\,(BL - CP)}{.25\,(H - L)}$$

Call Option A contract that gives the holder the right (but not the obligation) to buy a specific stock at a predetermined price on or before a certain date (called the expiration date).

Chicago Board Options Exchange (CBOE) The largest options exchange in the United States.

Covered Call A short call option position against a long position in the underlying stock or index.

Covered Put   A short put option position against a short position in the underlying stock or index.

European Style Option   An option contract that may be exercised only during a specified period of time just prior to its expiration.

Exercise   Implementing an option's right to buy or sell the underlying security.

Exercise Price   See strike price.

Expiration   The date and time after which an option may no longer be exercised.

Expiration Date   The last day on which an option may be exercised.

Fundamental Analysis   Evaluating a company to determine if it is a good investment risk. Evaluation is based mainly on balance sheet and income statements, past records of earnings, sales, assets, management, products and services.

Go Long   To buy securities or options.

Good 'Till Canceled Order (GTC)   Sometimes simply called *GTC* it means an order to buy or sell stock that is good until you cancel it.

Go Short   To sell securities or options.

Holder   One who purchases an option.

Index   An index is a group of stocks which can be traded as one portfolio, such as the S&P 500. Broad-based indexes cover a wide range of industries and companies and narrow-based indexes cover stocks in one industry or economic sector. Index Options   Call and put options on indexes of stocks that allow investors to trade in a specific industry group or market without having to buy all the stocks individually.

In-the-Money   An option is In-the-Money to the extent it has intrinsic value. (See Intrinsic Value). A call option is said to be In-the-Money when the price of the underlying stock is higher than the strike price of the option. A put option is said to be In-the-Money when the price of the underlying stock is lower than the strike price of the option.

Intrinsic Value A call option premium is said to have intrinsic value to the extent the stock price exceeds the strike price. A put option premium is said to have intrinsic value to the extent the strike price exceeds the stock price. The total value of the premium is intrinsic value (if any) plus the time value.

LEAPS (Long-term Equity AnticiPation Securities) Long dated options with expiration dates up to three years in the future.

Limit Order A condition on a transaction to buy at or below a specified price or to sell at or above a specified price.

Long A long position indicates that a stock, index, or option is owned.

Margin A loan by a broker to allow an investor to buy more stocks or options than available money (cash) in the account.

Margin Requirements (Options) The amount of cash an uncovered (naked) option writer is required to deposit and maintain to cover his daily position price changes.

Market Order An order that is filled immediately upon reaching the trading floor at the next best available price.

Naked Call See Uncovered Call

Naked Put See Uncovered Put

NASDAQ (National Association of Securities Dealers Automated Quotations) A computerized system providing brokers and dealers with price quotations for securities traded over-the-counter as well as for many New York Stock Exchange listed securities.

New York Stock Exchange (NYSE) The largest stock exchange in the United States.

Option   A security that represents the right, but not the obligation, to buy or sell a specified amount of an underlying security (stock, bond, futures contract, etc.) at a specified price within a specified time.

Option Class   A group of calls or a group of puts on the same stock.

Option Holder   The buyer of either a call or put option.

Option Premium   The price it costs to buy an option or the price paid for selling an option.

Option Series   Call or put options in the same class that have the same expiration date and strike price.

Option Writer   The seller of either a call or put option.

Out-of-the-Money   An option whose exercise price has no intrinsic value.

Out-of-the-Money Option (OTM)   A call option is out-of-the-money if its exercise or strike price is above the current market price of the underlying security. A put option is out-of-the-money if its exercise or strike price is below the current market price of the underlying security.

Premium   See Option Premium.

Price to Earnings Ratio (PE)   The current stock price divided by the earningsper share for the past year.

Put Factor   A formula to guide the selection of a naked put strike price and strike month. A factor greater than one is desirable. In the formula, PR is the naked put premium, SP is the strike price, CP is the current stock price, and ME is months to expiration.

$$\text{Put Factor} \ = \ \frac{6\,(100\,\text{PR})\,(\text{CP} - \text{SP})}{(\text{ME})\,(\text{SP})\,(\text{SP})}$$

Put Option A contract that gives the right (but not the obligation) to sell a specific stock at a predetermined price on or before a certain date (called the expiration date).

Security A trading instrument such as stocks, bonds, and short-term investments.

Short A short position indicates that a stock, index, or option is not owned.

Spread The price gap between the bid and ask price of a stock.

Stock A share of a company's stock translates into ownership of part of the company.

Stock Split An increase in the number of a stock's shares with a corresponding decrease in the par value of its stock.

Straddle A position consisting of a long call and a long put, or a short call and a short put, where both options have the same underlying security, strike price and expiration date.

Strangle A position consisting of a long call and a long put or a short call and a short put, where both options have the same underlying security, the same expiration date, but different strike prices.

Strike Price Also called the exercise price, is the price at which a call option holder can purchase the underlying stock by exercising the option, and is the price at which a put option holder can sell the underlying stock by exercising the option.

TAI—Take Action Indicator Formula for determining the relative attractiveness of stocks on the prospect list. In the formula BR is Buy Rank, FDA is Fifty Day Moving Average and CP is the current stock price.

$$TAI = BR \left(1 + \frac{FDA}{2(FDA) - CP} \right)$$

Technical Analysis   A method of evaluating securities and options by analyzing statistics generated by market activity, such as past high/low, up/down volume, momentum and moving averages.

Time Value   An option's premium consists of two parts: time value and intrinsic value. (See Intrinsic Value) The time value portion of the premium deteriorates with the passage of time and becomes zero with the expiration of the option.

Triple Witching Day   The third Friday in March, June, September and December when U.S. options, future options, and index options all expire on the same day.

Uncovered Call   A short call option in which the writer does not own the underlying security.

Uncovered Put   A short put option in which the writer does not have a corresponding short position on the underlying security.

Appendix

Now that you have gained the knowledge of "The Money Tree" concepts, your profits will be greatly enhanced by use of the following specially designed software programs. Free demonstration software can be downloaded from:

KellerPublishing.com

The Money Tree software for writing Covered Calls and Naked Puts provides a set of functions that allow you to quickly analyze prospective call and put option opportunities. The main program control panel is shown below that provides quick access to any feature.

The main functions and features are shown and described on the pages that follow.

The Buy Limit/Buy Rank Wizard allows you to quickly determine the current potential in any stock or index.

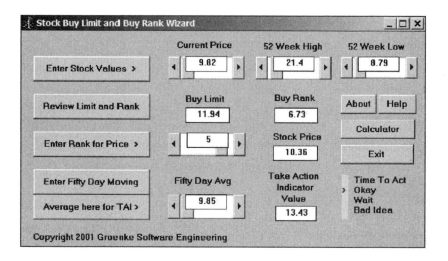

The Call Option Wizard guides you in the selection of the proper strike month and strike price for maximum gain as shown by the Magic Chart.

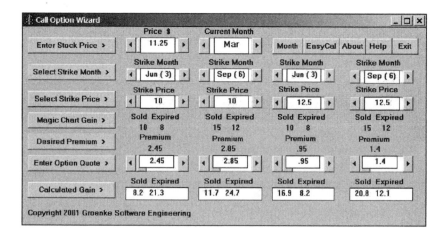

The Put Option Wizard calculates the Put Factor for any strike price and strike month combination. This factor then is used to show the premium desired in your selection analysis.

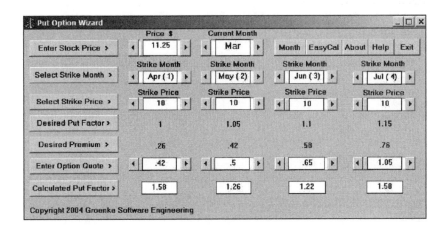

The calculator is handy for any small task.

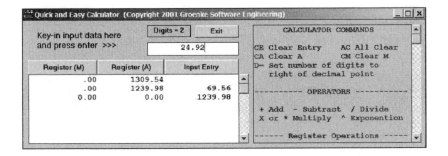

The Prospect List Manager (Stock PL Mgr) allows you to track your list of prospects. You can sort the list by Buy Rank (or any column) for quick analysis of the best opportunity.

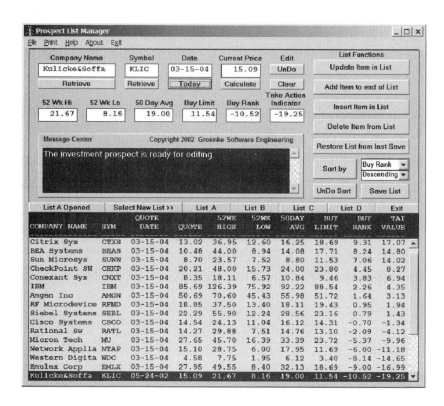

The Stock and Option Simulator allows you to review your plan for writing covered calls and naked puts. It gets you out of the dark and puts some light on the potential opportunities for your account. You can find out the difference between the potential gain for taxable and non-taxable accounts. Use it for covered calls or naked puts only or in any combination. This tool will show you how the compounding of option gains over time turns into excellent results in the long term.

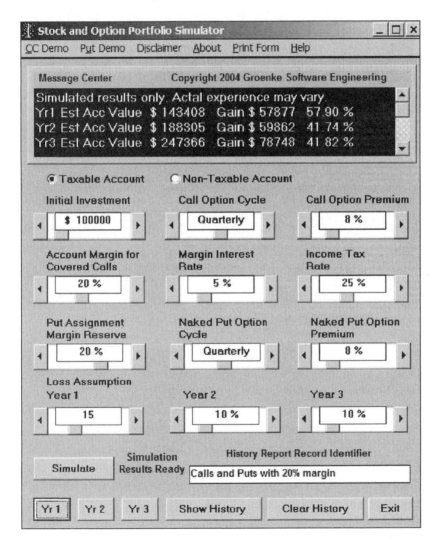

The Stock Market Simulator allows you to create your own picture of where the market may be headed. It is based on your own assessment of things such as interest rates, the employment picture, GDP growth, and other factors. Track your forecast against the actual market performance over time. Use it as a guide for investment decisions. The main program control panel, shown below, provides quick access to any feature.

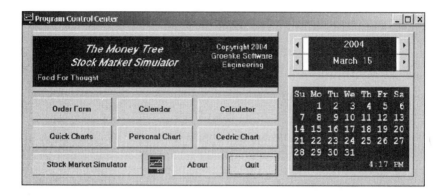

Use Quick Charts for a quick view of Rob Graham's or your own forecast of your favorite index or stock.

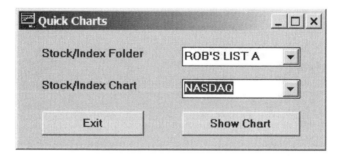

The Simulator page allows you to select the factors that may affect the market in the future. After the simulation is complete the forecast is displayed. After reviewing the results you can change your assumptions or view a graph of the day by day result. . The Tools sections allows you to update the actual numbers for tracking or with the Build feature (if purchased), you can build your own model of a stock or index.

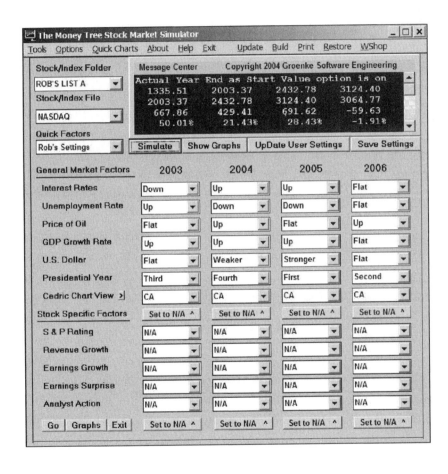

Here is a four year view for the factors selected. You can review
results by year or multiple years. You can export any chart in data
or bit map format.

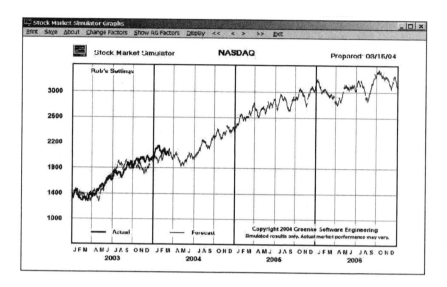

Here is a single year view.

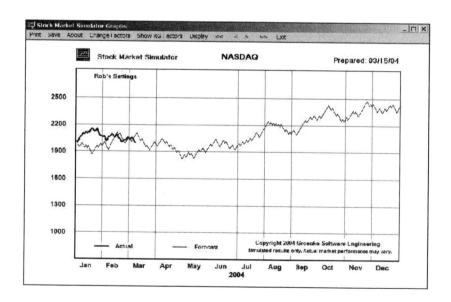

Here is the form that is used to build a model of a stock or index.
The step by step process guides you through the data input.

Build Data Base for Stock Market Simulator   _ □ ×

Restore   Exit

Here is the step by step process to create your own data base for the Stock Market Simulator. If at any time you do not want to continue go to Cancel. If you want to restore your User File back to the previous state then go to Oops. Otherwise select each step in succession to create your new entry.

Step 1   Enter a new Stock or Index name here >   NASDAQ

Step 2   Select type here >   ◯ Index   ◯ Stock

Step 3   Supply 253 daily closing price data points for the daily price change file. Enter data one item at a time followed by Enter or use (Ctrl C) in an Excel selected column of data and then (Ctrl V) in the data box followed by Update.

It is suggested that data starting at 1/2/02 be used. The simulator will forecast 2003 first and then future years.

Step 4   Supply the actual daily closing price starting with 1/2/03 up through today if possible. Copy the data from an Excel file if possible. Future updates can be made with the Update command on the main page. When done go to Next Step.

Step 5   Enter the 12/31/02 closing price here >

Step 6   Build forecasting equations with this command >   Find Equations

Step 7   Save file with this command >   Save Data

Step 8   You are now ready to simulate the market for your new entry. After you exit this Build form, select the Stock/Index name just created, set your factors and Simulate.   Done

Oops   If you think you made a mistake or do not want to keep your new entry you can restore your User File with this restore command. You are only allowed to go back one level for each Stock/Index addition. You can also change a new entry by again going through the Build process.   Restore

Stock/Index Folder Selected is: ROB'S LIST A   To cancel Build exit here >   Cancel

Here is the form that allows you to quickly update the actuals for any forecast. It allows you to copy data from any document with the copy (Ctrl C) and paste (Ctrl V) commands.

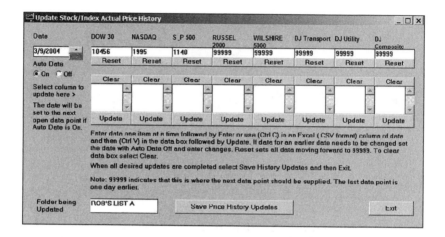

Create your own personal Bio-Rhythm chart with the Personal Chart function.

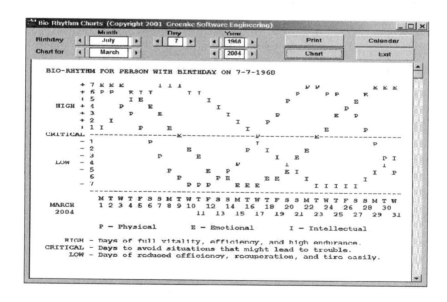

THE MAGIC CHART – SIDE ONE

MONTHS TO EXP.	IF SOLD	IF EXP.	JAN	FEB	MAR	APR	MAY	JUN
1	6.8	5.4	FEB	MAR	APR	MAY	JUN	JUL
2	8.4	6.7	MAR	APR	MAY	JUN	JUL	AUG
3	10.0	8.0	APR	MAY	JUN	JUL	AUG	SEP
4	11.6	09.3	MAY	JUN	JUL	AUG	SEP	OCT
5	13.4	10.7	JUN	JUL	AUG	SEP	OCT	NOV
6	15.0	12.0	JUL	AUG	SEP	OCT	NOV	DEC
7	16.6	13.3	AUG	SEP	OCT	NOV	DEC	JAN
8	18.4	14.7	SEP	OCT	NOV	DEC	JAN	FEB
9	20.0	16.0	OCT	NOV	DEC	JAN	FEB	MAR

THE MAGIC CHART – SIDE TWO

MONTHS TO EXP.	IF SOLD	IF EXP.	JUL	AUG	SEP	OCT	NOV	DEC
1	6.8	5.4	AUG	SEP	OCT	NOV	DEC	JAN
2	8.4	6.7	SEP	OCT	NOV	DEC	JAN	FEB
3	10.0	8.0	OCT	NOV	DEC	JAN	FEB	MAR
4	11.6	09.3	NOV	DEC	JAN	FEB	MAR	APR
5	13.4	10.7	DEC	JAN	FEB	MAR	APR	MAY
6	15.0	12.0	JAN	FEB	MAR	APR	MAY	JUN
7	16.6	13.3	FEB	MAR	APR	MAY	JUN	JUL
8	18.4	14.7	MAR	APR	MAY	JUN	JUL	AUG
9	20.0	16.0	APR	MAY	JUN	JUL	AUG	SEP

Book and Software Order Form

Mail this order form to:

Ship To:
Name _____

Keller Publishing
590 Fieldstone Dr.
Marco Island, FL 34145

Address _____

[Print]

City _____

[Exit]

Fax this form to: 1-239-642-9820

State/Zip _____

Call Toll Free 1-800-631-1952

Phone _____

Order and Download at
KellerPublishing.com

Email _____

Book	Cost	Qty	Total
Covered Calls and Naked Puts: Create Your Own Stock Options Money Tree.	$ 24.95 × _____		= $ _____

Software that implements the concepts in the book (See Appendix)

	Cost	Qty	Total
The Money Tree Software Tools for Writing Covered Calls and Naked Puts.	$ 24.95 × _____		= $ _____
The Money Tree Stock Market Simulator - Review where the market may go with your own outlook. (Includes forecast for 8 Indexes. Add up to 128 additional Indexes or Stocks).	$ 69.95 × _____		= $ _____
Excel Worksheets - Includes a Prospect List template, Option Plan template and Stock Transaction And History template.	$ 19.95 × _____		= $ _____
Special Offer: All three software items above.	$ 89.95 × _____		= $ _____

Subtotal _____

METHOD OF PAYMENT

FL Residents add 6% Sales Tax _____

_____ Check or money order payable to: KELLER PUBLISHING

Shipping / Handling $ 4.95

___ Visa ___ Mastercard ___ Amex   Account No:

TOTAL $ _____

— — — — — — — — — — — — — — —

Exp. Date _____

Delivered on CD for
Windows 95 and up.

Signature _____

Or Order and Download at
KellerPublishing.com

Thanks for your order. Please allow one week for delivery.

Ronald Groenke

RON GROENKE moved from Minnesota to the sunny gulf coast community of Marco Island after twenty-five years in the communications systems and software development environment. He has been active in the stock options market for eighteen years and developed the concepts and techniques provided in the book.

On Marco, he and wife, Jean, are active in their church and busy entertaining family and friends who visit from the north.

Besides options investing/advising, other activities include personal computing, Rotary, walking, boating, and traveling.

Ron can be reached at robgrahamphd@aol.com.